Battle Out c

GW01406648

Dwight V. Swain

Alpha Editions

This edition published in 2024

ISBN : 9789367247723

Design and Setting By
Alpha Editions
www.alphaedis.com
Email - info@alphaedis.com

Contents

CHAPTER I ....- 1 -

CHAPTER II...- 7 -

CHAPTER III ....- 20 -

CHAPTER IV ....- 31 -

CHAPTER V ....- 37 -

CHAPTER VI ....- 44 -

CHAPTER VII..- 50 -

CHAPTER VIII ....- 59 -

CHAPTER I

An utter dark lay upon the hills outside the palace now, moonless and with clouds drawn heavy all across the Cretan sky.

Wind, too, had come with the night, rising till Burke found himself fearing for the shutters. The lamps flared on their stands with each new gust and draft. Light flickered orange and yellow on Ariadne's lovely face, eddying through the shadows so that the tentacles of the frescoed octopi on the walls seemed to writhe and twist and turn....

Burke laughed without mirth. It was that mad a moment.

And that dangerous.

For while he might find temporary cover here with Ariadne, in these private quarters beyond the Queen's Megaron, death yet bayed at his heels.

Already, bearded King Minos himself no doubt paced some other palace hall—thirsting for Burke blood; raging in jealous fury that any outlander should dare aspire to his lovely daughter.

That slavering Greek lecher, Theseus, too—it was lucky he lay dead drunk there in the corner. Sober, and confronted with a rival, he'd kill just to salve his wounded ego.

And then, as if that were not enough of peril, there was ... the other.

Involuntarily, Burke shuddered.

What chance did a mere human have, pitted against the dark craft of the alien? Where could he hope to find the strength and skill and insight to win over the strange horror from beyond the void?

Yet with Ariadne's life at stake, Earth's whole future in the balance, how could he turn back?

No; he had no choice but to press on; seek out and challenge the might of that nightmare monster men called the Minotaur.

He couldn't help find it surprising, though, that in the face of such he still had it in him to notice the play of light on decorative motifs. Truly, the strange twist of mind that seemed to pervade this weird Mediterranean realm had claimed him for its own!

But to dare the Labyrinth, the Minotaur....

Almost without thinking, Burke rested a hand on the worn Smith & Wesson in his belt; then, bleakly, laughed again.

Ariadne moved uneasily beside him. Her words came halting and uncertain: "You—you are amused, my lord Dionysus...?"

Irritation boiled up in Burke—quick anger that he should have let himself forget even for a moment the desperate urgency of his task. How could he play the fool so—here, now, at a time when every breath, every second, brought inevitable disaster closer?

It added up to tension that had to find an outlet. Savagely, he lashed out at Ariadne: "For the hundredth time, girl: I'm not Dionysus, not a god. I'm Dion Burke, that's all. A man, like any other—"

Hurt came to the great dark eyes. A tear-mist veil blurred the glow of awe and adoration. The soft lips quivered.

But only for a moment. Then, contritely, the girl bowed her head. Jet ringlets glistened in the lamplight. Bringing up slim hands, she crossed them upon the firm young breasts that she wore bared in the traditional Minoan style. "Your pardon, my lord...."

Burke breathed in sharply. As swiftly as it had come, his anger died. Of a sudden he wanted nothing so much as to take the girl in his arms and draw her to him ... solace her, soothe her, hold her with a thousand tender caresses through the endless hours of this long, black night.

Why was it always so between him and Ariadne? What was there about this slim Minoan princess that the very sight of her should make his firmest resolves melt? The women he'd known in his own world—they'd been wiser, wittier; more beautiful, even, perhaps, by an objective standard. Yet not even the one who'd hurt him most and helped to precipitate him onto this fool's mission had stirred him a tenth as much as Ariadne.

With a curse, he reached out, pulled her to him.

She came willingly, nestling against him, her lithe body soft and warm.

For a long moment, Burke held her close.

Only then, over in the corner, brawny, bull-necked Theseus stirred and shifted. A noisy, wine-sodden snore broke from his open mouth.

Burke stiffened.

Like an echo, Ariadne's lovely oval face lifted from his shoulder. "My lord! You do not still feel anger—?"

Burke shook his head. "Forget it, princess. It's just I'm all on edge. There's not much time—"

He broke off; brought up his wrist and strained to read the watch-face.

And that was good for another wry, twisted shadow of smile: a watch, here in Bronze Age Crete ... product of the United States of America, vintage 1954 A. D., wrenched 5,000 miles and 3300 years out of its place and time. An anachronism to end all anachronisms.

Or no, that wasn't quite true.

For surely he himself was a greater anachronism than the watch, even.

The bare facts alone would drive an obituary writer crazy: "Dion Burke, archaeologist extraordinary without portfolio; born, Erie, Pa., August 9, 1929; disappeared April 14, 1957; died at Knossos, in the Great Palace of Minos, mightiest sea-king of Crete, on some vague, early spring date in the vicinity of 1400 B. C."

Only no obituary writer would ever hear those facts. The watch, the gun, the lighter—they'd all have sifted away to rusty dust long before Sir Arthur Evans and his fellow-scholars came this way.

Not that that mattered. Not now; not while he still had a job to do.

He moved his wrist closer to the nearest of the flickering lamps, and strained again to read the watch.

Almost 10:30. Little more than an hour-and-a-half till midnight and the moment of Knossos' doom.

Sometime between now and then, he had to meet the Minotaur.

For a moment he held the slim girl in his arms even closer than before. Then, ever so gently, he moved her back away a fraction; lifted her small, satin-smooth chin. "Ariadne...."

"Yes, my lord?"

"There's a thing I must do now, Ariadne. An important thing, for both of us." A pause. "I need your help to do it."

"My help—?" The dark eyes widened. "My lord knows he has only to command. What must I do?"

Carefully, Burke picked his words; strove to hold the tension from his voice: "Among the people of this palace, there's one called Daedalus. You know him?"

"Daedalus the Smith, you mean?" The jet ringlets danced as the girl laughed. "Of course I know him. He's chief of all my father's craftsmen. What is it you seek of him?"

Again, Burke weighed his words. "Some talk, that's all. A chance to ask a few questions."

"Talk—at this hour?" Ariadne stared.

"I have no choice," Burke shrugged. "To see him by daylight would be as much as my life is worth."

"Oh."

"Yes." Time for a smile now, Burke decided. His most engaging smile. "You see, there are things the man knows, things his skill's taught him—"

Ariadne stiffened in the same instant. "Things Daedalus knows—?" For the first time, her voice held an edge, dark shadows of suspicion. "How could a smith know anything that means so much? What might he say that my lord Dion had not already heard a thousand times?"

"What—?" Burke felt his smile go stiff. "Why—why, many things—his skills, his artifices—" He groped and fumbled.

"No!" In a flash all Ariadne's humility of manner vanished. She thrust Burke's restraining arm aside, defiance in the gesture. "Do you think me a fool, my lord Dion? Daedalus the Smith holds but one secret that such as you might seek to learn. One only!"

Burke stood ever so still.

Ariadne spat like a cat. "You seek the secret of the Labyrinth, my lord! You would stalk the Minotaur in his very lair! Waste no breath trying to lull me with denials!"

Burke sighed. A weary sigh, heavy with the knowledge of all the things he could not change.

And, from Ariadne: "What makes you think you're destined to succeed, where each year fourteen others fail? How dare you hope to live, when the monster that is the Minotaur has slain the mightiest warriors of all Athens?"

How, indeed? Of a sudden, Burke wanted no more of such questions.

He cut in flat and hard: "Shut up, wench!"

The girl stopped as short as if he'd slapped her. Her face paled with anger.

Only then, as she stared up at Burke, that too passed, and a mask of sudden fear came to replace the fury. Her naked breasts lifted with a quick, indrawn breath. She fell back an uncertain step ... another ... another.... "My lord—Dionysus—"

Burke laughed harshly. "All right. Call me that if you want to." And then, tight-lipped: "Because make up your mind to it, you're going to do what I say as if I were your whole damn' pantheon!"

He closed in.

The girl pressed back against the wall now—white to the lips, dark eyes distended. "Dion—Dion Burke—"

Burke gripped her wrist. "Is it agreed, then? You'll do what I tell you?"

His lovely captive winced as he twisted. "But—my lord—the Minotaur—Dion, it will slay you!"

"Maybe. And then again, maybe not." Burke brushed a hand against the revolver in his waistband. "You see, I won't be on quite the same spot as those others who died, Ariadne. I've reserved a couple of special Dionysan thunderbolts to try out on your monster, patent of two subsidiary gods named Smith & Wesson."

"But Daedalus—he's my father's man, Lord Dion, chief of all the palace craftsmen. He'd never help you, even if you could reach him."

"I'll reach him. And he'll help me."

"But why, my lord? Why risk it?" A sudden taut, eager note crept into Ariadne's voice. With her free hand, she smoothed the fabric of Burke's shirt. "Don't you see? There's no need—not when you've the power to come here as you have tonight, in spite of all my father's guards! Under his very sword, we can be lovers—"

Burke smiled bleakly. "I'm sorry, princess. I wish it were that simple."

"But it is!" Now Ariadne's lithe young body once more was tight against his. "I want you to come, my lord Dion! I welcome you—"

"I know. And ... I love you too." For the fraction of a second Burke let his arms tighten around her.

Then, abruptly, he pushed back; gripped her shoulders. "You see, I can't just come and go at will, the way you seem to think I can. And even if I could, it wouldn't help."

"It would not—?" Blank bafflement spread across Ariadne's lovely face.

"Not after tonight."

Puzzled eyes. A wordless question.

Burke said tightly, "By tomorrow there won't be any Knossos. The Great Palace here, the shrines, the other buildings—as of midnight tonight, less than an hour-and-a-half from now, they'll all be destroyed."

Tension, spiraling higher with each passing second.

Burke said, "Now you know why I came tonight, Ariadne: because this is the last chance I'll ever have. I've got to get you out of here, now or never. That's why I have to see Daedalus, and go into the Labyrinth, and meet the Minotaur and kill it."

Still the silence echoed.

A numb despair seeped through Burke. Bleakly, he wondered how he ever had been fool enough to think his words might spark response in a Bronze Age mind, or that any such mad enterprise as this could possibly end otherwise than in disaster.

Only then, while he watched, once more Ariadne bowed her head and crossed her hands upon her breasts. Her words came low, submissive: "The quarters of Daedalus the Smith lie close at hand, my lord."

She turned as she spoke.

Heart pounding, Burke walked with her towards the doorway....

CHAPTER II

There was a guard in the corridor beyond the Queen's Megaron.

Wordless, Burke flicked a glance at Ariadne.

Her dark eyes flashed a daredevil acceptance of the challenge. Sliding past him, she swung the heavy door back so it hid him, then leaned against it, body arched in practiced coquetry.

The spearman outside straightened just a fraction. His chest swelled and his belly drew in.

Slowly, Ariadne's full lips curved in a smile that was all invitation. Her hand came up to smooth her hair as she turned, twisting and preening. Then, still unspeaking, and with one last lingering glance over her shoulder, she drew back into her own apartment.

The guard's head swiveled as his eyes followed her.

Ariadne laughed softly from the shadows. Her long skirt swirled and rustled.

The guard's breath rasped in the stillness. For an instant he hesitated, peering down the hall in both directions. Then, eagerly, he crossed the threshold and moved with swift steps towards the princess.

Burke waited till the man was clear of the door. Then, savagely, the Smith & Wesson flat on the palm of his hand, he stepped forth from his hiding place and smashed a blow to the back of the other's neck.

The guard's knees hinged. He spilled to the floor.

Burke snapped, "Quick! Cords! A gag!"

The shrill, nerve-jangling squeal of cloth tearing echoed. Deftly, Ariadne thrust strips from a drape into his hands.

Burke bound and gagged the guard, then straightened and strode across the room to where bull-necked, snoring Theseus lay, the stench of sour wine still thick about him.

Ariadne came close. "More cloth, my lord?"

Burke prodded the Greek ungently with his toe, without response; then once more glanced at his watch.

Ten forty-five now.

And that left only an hour-and-a-quarter more, at best.

The back of Burke's neck prickled. "Forget it," he clipped. "The Hero of Athens is too drunk to turn over, even, let alone give us trouble."

"This way, then," the girl said. Her voice all at once was not too steady, and the hand that gripped Burke's showed a tendency to tremble.

Together, they made their way from the apartment, down the corridor past a row of great painted jars and, finally, out onto the long ascending ramp that led to the palace's central court.

Now Ariadne turned right, keeping to the shadows of the colonnaded buildings past which they moved.

Close behind her, gun in hand, Burke tried to watch all ways at once. Every rattling stone, every wind-tossed branch against the cloud-blocked sky, became for him a trigger for new tension. Once, when the shadows behind him flickered, he almost persuaded himself that Theseus must be on their heels. Or perhaps, somehow, they'd caught the attention of another of old Minos' guards....

Again Ariadne veered right. A door creaked as she put her shoulder to it.

This corridor was so black Burke had to grip the girl's hand to keep contact with her.

More doors. More halls. More rooms. The place was like a maze—the very Labyrinth itself.

Yet not once did Ariadne hesitate. Swift, sure, she led Burke on and on through one murky chamber after another.

Then, as they rounded a final corner, a block of greyness came to mark the end of a passage. In seconds, they were once more out into the open and the night.

Ariadne paused and pointed. "That's the place," she whispered.

"Daedalus' quarters?"

"Yes."

Narrow-eyed, Burke studied the looming bulk a moment. Then, tight-lipped, he strode towards the geometric shadows that marked the entrance.

But now Ariadne caught his arm. "Please, my lord Dion—let me be the one to talk to Daedalus."

"Let you—?" Burke stared. "But why?"

"You wish him to speak, do you not—to tell you the things you seek to learn?"

"Do I want him to talk—?" Burke spoke between clenched teeth. "Believe me, it's more than that, Princess. He's got to!"

The girl laughed softly in the darkness; and somehow there was a ring of steel beneath the velvet. "That's why I must be the one to face him, Lord Dion!"

Without waiting for further word from Burke, she stepped forward and knocked upon the door.

No answer. After a moment, she knocked again.

This time, a faint stir of sound rose from within. Then, abruptly, the door opened, framing a brawny, bearded man who glowered out at Burke and the girl from below a sputtering, hand-held lamp.

Uncowed, without hesitation, Ariadne stepped forward. "Come, Daedalus!" she chided smoothly. "Would you leave your master's daughter standing here wind-whipped on your threshold in the night?"

The belligerence vanished from Daedalus' face, replaced by an impassive, noncommittal mask. For an instant his eyes flicked to Burke. Then he stepped back heavily; opened the door wider. "Enter, my princess. What brings you to my poor quarters at this hour of the night?"

Uninvited, ignoring the hostility that gleamed in their host's deep-set eyes, Burke followed Ariadne in and closed the door behind them.

Simultaneously, the girl said, "It was a terrible thing for you to do, Daedalus! Did my father know it, he'd have you flayed alive!"

Even Burke rocked back on his heels: the words were that much of a shock, that unexpected ... cool, conversational, without preliminary.

As for the smith, he stood very still. The deep-set eyes seemed to retreat yet further into the broad, high-domed skull.

"And what is this terrible thing of which you speak, Princess Ariadne?" he asked finally.

"What is it—?" Ariadne's eyes distended, then narrowed. Her voice took on a taut, dangerous note. "Do you think to mock me, artisan? Me, daughter of Minos, favored beyond all women of this realm?"

Daedalus' hairy chest rose and fell in heavy, almost deliberate rhythm. Turning, he crossed with short, clumping steps to the nearest stand and set down his lamp, then made a small business of straightening the wick.

"What black slander is this, princess?" he asked coldly, eyes still on the flame. "What are you trying to say I've done?"

"Would you deny it, then?" Like a sleek cat stalking, Ariadne moved round him in a long, slow arc. "Or do you seek perhaps to saddle poor Icarus with the blame?"

"Icarus—!" The smith's head lifted sharply. "Whatever this deed is that you speak of, my son had nothing to do with it!"

"Do you count it nothing for a youth to enter secretly into my apartment, then assault a guard when he's surprised?" Ariadne's lovely face fixed into a mask of scorn. "Ambition ill becomes you, Daedalus. For a man who'd plot such a thing, risk his own son's life to gain power over me, you show little courage and less sense."

Before Burke's eyes, sweat came to the smith's broad forehead. A tremor ran through the heavy hands. "May the gods bear witness, Ariadne, you know I've done no such, and so does your father!"

"And of course he'll take your word over his own daughter's." Ariadne laughed without mirth. "Tell me, smith, are you such a fool as to think your fiend's work with my mother, Pasiphae, is so soon forgotten?" And then: "Besides, you know all the secrets of the palace—a dangerous knowledge. My father will leap at an excuse to slay you!"

Daedalus rubbed at his beard with thick, scarred knuckles. His lips had a dry, parched look, and his breathing was ragged and uneven.

Coolly, Ariadne turned and walked away from him, to Burke. "Come, my lord Dion! Let us waste no more time on this numb-skull."

Daedalus' head seemed to sink down between his great shoulders. Through clenched teeth, he said, "All right, curse you! What is it you want?"

"What do you mean, smith?" The girl stayed remote as some slim statue. "Are your wits slipping? You know I've asked for nothing."

Head high, a picture of poise, she moved towards the door. Stiffly, Burke fell in behind her.

For a moment, Daedalus stood flat-footed, rigid.

Then, abruptly, he too was moving towards the door. For the first time, his voice held a raw, uncertain edge, as if touched with panic. "Princess—most favored of Minos—please—"

Ariadne paused. Her dark eyes glinted soaring triumph in the instant that they touched Burke's. "Please indeed, Daedalus! After all, I came here tonight but to satisfy a whim. This outlander,"—a gesture to Burke—"vows there's no access to the Labyrinth, the Minotaur, save by the Shrine of Oracles.

"For my part, I argued that you, who laid out that whole area of the palace, could enter any chamber, no matter how well the doors were guarded." A shrug. "All the talk—it ended in a wager. So, now, I count on you to prove me right, show some secret way by which, if necessary, a determined man could invade even the Minotaur's most secret precinct undetected."

The beads of sweat on the smith's broad forehead began to merge into rills and trickle down into his eye-brows. "Princess, were I to tell this outlander such a secret—believe me, you ask me to gamble with my life!"

"Yet if you do not tell," Ariadne retorted calmly, "what will happen will involve no gamble!"

———————————

Seconds ticked by while the heavy-thewed chief of craftsmen stared at her. Then, bleakly, he said, "Very well, princess."

Another long pause, with Daedalus frowning and tugging at his lower lip.

At last: "The only unguarded way to the Minotaur leads through the drainage system, the great sewer-pipes that lie beneath the palace."

Burke frowned. "You mean, you'd drop through a manhole here—anywhere on the grounds—and then come up again inside the Labyrinth?"

"Exactly," the smith nodded.

"But how would you know when you reached the right exit?"

"Only one connects with the Labyrinth. A cage of bars cuts off the pipe at that point, so no workman may by accident come up within the Labyrinth and thus meet his doom."

Narrow-eyed, Burke brooded on the things the smith had told him.

But now Ariadne broke in; and all the poise she'd shown brief moments earlier had vanished: "Dion—you mustn't! Don't you see? This is a trap. Even though you were to slay the Minotaur, you'd never find your way back to safety through all that maze of pitch-black tunnels!"

"On the contrary, princess." Burke smiled thinly. "This is one advantage of coming here from another time. It tells me in advance so many of the things that are scheduled to happen."

Ignoring her obvious blank bafflement, he again spoke to the smith: "Daedalus, do you have cord here—light, strong line such as you use in laying out the walls of each new building?"

"Yes."

"Then get some for me."

The brawny craftsman crossed to a chest against the wall; brought out a thick skein of twine. "Will this do?"

"Is it long enough to guide me to the Labyrinth?"

"Yes."

"Then that's all I need from you." Burke turned to go.

"Wait!" This from Ariadne. Her dark eyes pinned their host's deep-set orbs. "Daedalus, I've a promise to make you."

"A promise—?"

"A vow, if you will." Never had Ariadne looked more beautiful—or more deadly. Her smile held the shadow of impending doom. "For if there's any trick to this, smith, or if word should reach my father of what's happened here tonight, I swear an hour will come when you'll pray for death to end your agonies!"

Then she and Burke were out in the night again, silent as shadows, feeling their way back through the murky maze of alleyways and corridors and buildings to the central court.

Burke pulled the girl to a halt there, in the narrow slot between two pillars. "Where are we going?" He held his voice low; spoke with his mouth close to her ear to compensate for the buffeting of the wind. "We can't chance your rooms, you know. That guard's snapped out of it by now."

"Of course. I've a place in mind across the court, closer to the shrine."

"All right, then."

But again, as before, tension rose within Burke. A guard's shouted challenge somewhere far off started him sweating. When the low, mingled laughter of a man and a woman drifted from a nearby window, he froze in his tracks.

The role of hero, he decided, ill became him. He thought too much of consequence and peril; found it too difficult to lose himself in an emotional haze of recklessness.

Yet here, now, he had no choice—not feeling the way he did about Ariadne; not knowing the things he knew from that brief session before the inverter's scanning screen.

And the time remaining was so short ... less than an hour, as of this moment.

"This way, my lord Dion."

Wordless, once more Burke fell in behind the girl.

Their destination proved to be an ornate suite where Burke stumbled over furniture in the darkness.

Ariadne squeezed his hand. "No one will disturb us here—those who occupy this apartment are visiting at Phaestos." And then, changing position: "I've a lamp. Give me fire."

Burke fumbled out his lighter; flicked the wheel.

The flame showed his companion close beside him. In seconds, the lamp she held was sputtering to life.

The girl turned quickly. "There's a manhole back here, in the ante-room to the bath."

She led Burke to it as she spoke; held the lamp low so he could see the cover-slab.

Dropping to his knees, he heaved the heavy stone aside.

Instantly, new air-currents swirled about him. A mustiness assailed his nostrils.

Somewhere, along that black tube below or another like it, the Minotaur was waiting.

A knot drew tight in the pit of Burke's stomach. Rising, he tossed Daedalus' thick skein of cord down by the base of the nearest lamp-stand, then faced Ariadne.

"Thank you for your help, my princess," he said gently. "Now, though, it's time for you to go."

"To go—?" She stared at him, dark eyes suddenly wide. "What byplay is this, my lord Dion? Surely you'd not ask me to leave you now, in the hour when your worst danger is upon you?"

Burke forced a wry smile. "Do you remember what happened the other time when you refused to carry out my orders?"

"You mean—when you hit me?" Gingerly, the girl's fingers moved along her bruised jaw as she spoke.

"Precisely."

"But my lord Dion—"

Burke stopped smiling. "I'm sorry, Ariadne. You're not going with me. That's final. If you try, if you won't promise to go back to your own apartment, I'll knock you out and tie you up. Is that clear?"

He started forward as he finished—face set, fist doubled.

But the girl gave not an inch before him. Stepping in, instead, she stood very close, face upturned to his.

"My lord Dion," she said softly, "I tell you now: you're the bravest man I've ever seen."

It threw Burke off balance. He could find no words with which to answer.

The girl said, "I promise you, you needn't worry for me; a warrior should not have to think of women, or fear for them. I'll await you at my own apartment."

Burke groped. "Ariadne—"

It was as if he hadn't spoken: "Remember, you have my promise. But if anything should go wrong, if I'm missing when you reach my quarters— Lord Dion, do you know the River of Amnissus?"

"Yes, of course."

"To its left, where it meets the sea, a headland rises. So, if fate decrees that I must flee from Knossos, you can expect to find me there."

Her slim, soft arms were round his neck, then; her lips on his for a long, pulsing moment.

When it ended, she was sobbing, her cheeks tear-streaked.

"Dion ..." she choked. "Please my Lord Dion, come back to me! Without you—"

She broke off; whirled and fled.

For a long, long moment, Burke stared after her, straining his eyes against the black encroachment of the night.

Then, abruptly, he dropped to one knee and set to looping one end of Daedalus' cord around the lamp-stand—tying it tight; tugging and testing it.

Sound stirred behind him, a faint whisper.

Burke bit down hard. "Damn you, Ariadne!"

No answer.

Another fragment of sound. A footstep.

A footstep far too heavy to be Ariadne's.

Burke went rigid; started to turn.

Only before he could even bring his eyes up, something clouted him a terrific blow to the side of the head, so hard it knocked him clear off his feet and against the wall beside him.

Desperately, he tried to roll clear, get his gun out.

But his eyes blurred. His head rang. A sandaled foot kicked the Smith & Wesson out of his fumbling fingers before the weapon had hardly cleared his waistband.

And now, a tremendous weight crashed down upon him. Blows rained to his face, his rib-cage, his belly. A knee drove for his groin. Cable-muscled fingers clutched his windpipe.

Burke choked on his own tongue. The fingers cut off his breath. His head spun. His chest heaved—lungs aflame, convulsing in agony.

Then spidery tendrils of blackness seeped into his brain. His will to fight ebbed. He felt himself drifting away, as on a swift-flowing stream that plunged into a cave's dark, swirling shadows.

Cautiously, the fingers relaxed on his windpipe.

Burke fought for breath in short, tremulous gasps. He didn't have the strength in him even to fill his lungs fully, let alone try to renew the battle.

The fingers left his throat and fumbled at his wrists; then his ankles.

Burke began to get better control of his breathing. Forcing himself to ignore his aching head and battered body, he pried his eyes open.

Bull-necked Theseus squatted by his side, leering down at him. The Greek gripped the Smith & Wesson in one hand, and every line of his face and stance mirrored gloating triumph.

Cold with rage—or was it partly panic?—Burke stared up at his captor. But when he tried to move his arms to lift himself, he found that they were bound together.

Beside him, the Athenian chuckled unpleasantly. "That Minos is smart, isn't he?"

Burke stared. "Minos—?"

"Sure. He told me I'd catch you if I just played drunk long enough." The other's smirk broadened. "That's how much he hates you, see? He said he'd let me and the others go, forget all that crazy stuff with the Minotaur. All I had to do was grab you before you could sneak away someplace with Ariadne."

It was all Burke could do to keep from groaning.

If Theseus noticed, he ignored it. "Me, I've got a better idea. Something really clever. You'll love it."

A small chill ran through Burke. He still didn't speak.

Theseus said, "You want to get at the Minotaur so rotten much—well, I'm just the boy to help you do it, now you've worked all the details out with that Daedalus and Ariadne." A leer. "We'll handle it just the way you planned it: drop into the sewer-tunnel here, then hunt till we find the manhole into the Labyrinth."

The burly Greek got up as he finished. "All right. On your feet!"

By way of emphasis, he kicked Burke in the stomach.

Retching, Burke lurched over to a face-down position and tried to rise.

Stumbling erect proved difficult enough. Then, on his feet at last, he discovered that his captor had hobbled his ankles also, so he could move only in short, awkward steps.

Now the Athenian gestured to the open manhole that led into the sewer. "Hurry it up! Get down there!"

Awkwardly, Burke shuffled towards the opening.

Apparently he moved too slowly for his captor's tastes, for a sandaled foot took a leg from under him and he spilled to the floor and half-fell through the hole.

Then he was down in the cool, drafty blackness of the great drain. A moment later, Theseus joined him, a lamp in one hand, Daedalus' cord in the other. The revolver he'd taken from Burke was thrust into his loin-band.

Together, with Burke pushed into the lead, they moved along the tunnel.

It was a nightmare, after that—a nightmare of slime and smells, sudden winds and water. Snakes slithered across Burke's feet. Cobwebs brushed his face. The lamp's gleam was a pinprick in an infinity of darkness. A dozen times they struck dead ends; retraced their steps out of blind alleys. And each time Theseus raged with greater fury, till Burke's back and hips were numb with blows and kicks and buffets.

And then, suddenly, they came to a place where a cage of bars blocked off the passage.

Burke's heart leaped. A tight band seemed to constrict his chest.

But before he could even speak, Theseus elbowed him aside with new blows and curses. The Hero of Athens was breathing hard; even by the lamp's feeble light, his eyes showed distended.

Looping the heavy skein of twine over his shoulder, the Greek now gripped the nearest bar in a brawny hand and shook it.

It didn't even quiver.

Snarling, Theseus stepped back and, lifting the lamp, scrutinized the terra cotta of the tunnel wall till he found a crack-formed ledge wide enough to hold the light. Then, returning to the bars, he seized one in both hands and heaved on it while he braced a foot against another.

Still nothing happened.

Again the Athenian heaved, and this time every muscle along his back and arms and legs swelled. His belly drew into heavy ridges. Veins stood out at throat and temple.

For the instant, even Burke couldn't help but watch fascinated at the picture of sheer physical strength displayed.

And now, ever so slowly, one of the bars began to bend ... the merest fraction ... an inch ... a hand's breadth....

Then, suddenly, with a dull metallic twang, the piece tore loose from its fitting.

The sound broke Burke's spell. Convulsively, he strained at the bonds that held his own wrists.

They only cut deeper into the flesh.

And there was so little time....

Warily, Burke cast a sidewise glance at the revolver, still hanging at the other's waist. Then, as casually as he could manage it, he started moving closer.

Now, panting with exertion, Theseus turned his attention to a second bar.

This time, he had more room to maneuver. Almost from the first moment, the metal showed signs of twisting.

Burke took yet another sidling step—a step that brought him within arm's reach of the Smith & Wesson. Clumsily, he poised, readying himself to spear out for the butt with both hands as one.

A groan escaped Theseus as he wrenched at the reluctant bar with all his might. Little by little, the heavy metal bent.

Burke snatched for the gun.

Only as he did so, incredibly, the weapon wasn't there. His hands slapped Theseus' sweat-greased side instead.

Simultaneously, a fist like a maul smashed him full in the face: The Athenian's harsh laughter rang in his ears. He crashed back against the sewer-pipe's wall like a doll flung aside by an angry child. Words hammered at him; Theseus' words: "I wondered when you'd try that, you outlander dog!"

It was all Burke could do to keep his feet, let alone answer.

The Greek snarled, "Now's a good time to tell you the rest of it, too, rack you!"

Burke tried to blink away the haze between them. "The rest of it—?" he mumbled.

"That's right; the rest." His captor gloated openly now. "You didn't think I dragged you through this hell-hole just for entertainment, did you, when all I needed to do to get rid of you was hand you over to Minos?"

Burke didn't answer.

Theseus scowled, spoke almost as if to himself; "That slut Ariadne—I'll teach her to scorn me for an outlander! Once I've shoved you up through this manhole into the Labyrinth, where there's no chance for anyone but the Minotaur to find you, alive or dead, I'm going to go explain to Minos all about how you took me unawares and almost killed me, back there in Ariadne's quarters. He'll believe me, because it fits right in with what that guard you tricked will tell him.

"Then, while Minos has everyone out hunting for you, I'll take Ariadne down to where my ship lies anchored at the mouth of the Amnissus. By the time Minos realizes what's happened, I'll be gone, with his daughter with me; and she'll be good for nothing but to be queen of Athens, so he'll have no choice but to make peace with my father, no matter how it galls him."

The hair along the back of Burke's neck prickled. Of a sudden he saw how he'd vastly underestimated Theseus. Because the man looked like a handsome, stupid, dissipated block of beef, Twentieth Century intellect had sneered at him.

Only Theseus had a schemer's brain, as well as a Greek God's face and physique. And what looked like stupidity came out as an almost oriental taste for the un-prettier types of vengeance.

All of which added up to nothing less than disaster.

Keeping his voice level with an effort, Burke said, "Theseus, you hate me, and I don't blame you for it. For that matter, I hate you too.

"But right now, there's no time for either of us to indulge his feelings. This is too big for that. Knossos falls tonight. It's going to be destroyed—soon now, within the hour.

"Unless we kill the Minotaur, Ariadne dies too. There'll even be other Minotaurs, not just here but all over the world. That's why I wanted to get into the Labyrinth—"

Laughter exploded in Burke's face.

It was a better answer than words. Tight-lipped, Burke groped frantically for some new plan, some trick, some lingering straw of hope to cling to.

Theseus said, "Don't worry, outlander. You'll get your chance at the Minotaur."

He stalked forward as he spoke; poised a doubled fist close by Burke's jaw. "Just remember, though: while you're taking care of the monster, I'll be taking care of Ariadne!"

The poised fist lashed out. When Burke tried to jerk his head aside, Theseus' other hand came up in a casual, almost lazy arc and slapped it back into place.

Fist and jaw met. Burke's brain exploded inside his skull. The flickering lamp seemed to burst into a blaze of dazzling, kaleidoscopic stars.

Then, one by one, they faded. Blackness closed in....

CHAPTER III

The feeling, Burke decided, basically was one of frustration—a moiling, roiling, boiling tension that crept higher and higher as his own helplessness became the more apparent.

Well, what else could he expect, in a situation sprung from monomania's loins? From the beginning, everything about this business had had the spell of madness on it. Success, when the cards were down, had always been too much to hope for.

Now, thinking of it, Burke could only sigh bleakly and shake his head.

Only that wasn't quite true, either. For his head wouldn't shake, and his sigh held neither sound nor breath.

How had it all come about, this nightmare? Where had it started, really?

With the Research Professor?

With The Girl?

With The Director?

But no. In his heart Burke knew that none of them held the answer.

Because the beginning lay farther back ... so much, much farther....

... All the way back to the old, dormer-windowed house amid the elms, and his childhood, and the Bowl of Minos.

The bowl....

He could still remember the first time he saw it, lying in a litter-heaped trunk up in the attic.

Fascinated, he'd picked it up and run stubby fingers over the stylized Minoan octopus that stood out in bold relief upon its surface, till it seemed he could almost feel the twining tentacles' pressure.

It brought a queer sense of excitement to him ... a sort of paradox of feeling that made him thrill to the bowl's beauty even while he stared at the creature that served as its decoration with a strange, shuddery sensation close akin to horror.

Then his mother saw what he was doing, and took the pottery vessel from him, explaining the while about the footloose, adventuring uncle who'd brought it here all the way from Crete.

A lump formed in Burke's throat as he recalled her patience ... how when she'd found him returning again and again to the attic and the trunk, she'd brought the bowl down and given it a place on the livingroom table, where he could examine it all at will.

Someone even told him about Minos and Theseus and Pasiphae and Ariadne and the Minotaur, and all the rest of the legendry that went with Bronze Age Crete.

Yet the legends were never quite enough. They raised too many questions; left too much unsaid.

The fragments of fact he picked up proved even less satisfactory.

How had a civilization rich and powerful and advanced as that of the Minoans ever risen on a sea-isolated island such as Crete?

Where had the Minoans learned their skills, their arts?

Above all, why had their culture vanished? What brought about Great Knossos' fall?

Questions without answers, all of them. Mysteries like the Cretan's strange, undeciphered writing, and the final fate of lovely Princess Ariadne, Minos' daughter, and how Theseus, bare-handed, could have slain the mighty Minotaur.

It was all enough to drive a seven-eight-nine-ten-year-old boy to distraction!

Then a careless visitor's elbow knocked the bowl to the floor. It shattered into shards.

At ten, a boy's too old to cry—before company, at least. So he'd clenched his fists behind his back, and blinked back the tears, and held his mouth to a stiff white line till he could be alone, face pillow-muffled, behind the closed door of his room.

And from that moment he'd known that sometime, somehow, he himself would find his way to Crete.

School became a place where he greedily snatched up crumbs of mythology and history between dreary hours spent battling his way through all the other subjects his teachers demanded that he learn.

High school brought a broader view. He began to see the interrelatedness of learning. Literature, chemistry, physics, Latin—of a sudden he found he loved them all.

Yet always, always, there ahead lay Knossos, beckoning.

How old had he been when, avidly, he plowed his way through Sir Arthur Evans' "Palace of Minos", groping his way by context past all the unfamiliar words? Thirteen? Fourteen?

By high school commencement time, he no longer cared that his parents couldn't understand his passion for things Cretan.

College, then. Major in anthropology, minor in classics. Greek now, as well as Latin. Linguistics, too. Comparative cultures, technical photography, ethnological methods, archaeological methods, museum methods. Year after year, course after course.

And always, the same goal. Let others weigh and choose between Yucatan and Oceania, Murdering Beach and the Valley of the Kings. For him—ever; always—there was only Minos and Knossos and Bronze Age Crete.

Dion Burke, B.A., now, Dion Burke, M.A.

Then, the last step; the final goal: the onward, upward march to Doctor of Philosophy, Ph.D.

Or rather, not quite: not quite Ph.D.

And that was where The Director came in.

Burke cursed the day he'd met him.

A kindly soul, The Director, by his own statement, in spite of his scowl and beetling brows and jutting, heavy-boned, prognathous jaw. So fascinated by all things Minoan. So happy such a brilliant student had selected this most benign of all universities as the one at which to work for his doctorate.

It was only a step from there to casual acquaintance with The Research Professor.

The Professor was the first universally-acknowledged-as-authentic genius Burke had even known. Even the man's colleagues on the staff of the university's Science Institute agreed that he knew more about certain aspects of electronics than anyone alive.

The Professor, it developed, wanted Burke's collaboration on a project—a device he termed a "computational translator" which he felt might solve the riddle of the mysterious Minoan language, if only its hieroglyphics could somehow be reduced to sound.

That was when Burke brought out his own idea, his madman's dream for the ultimate archaeological tool.

An inverter, he called it; a time inverter, designed to carry researchers back bodily into the past.

The Professor scoffed openly when Burke first told him about it.

The second time, he frowned and tugged at his pointed chin.

The third found him already at work.

The computational translator, and the time inverter. Two lunatic concepts, born of monomania and genius.

Two concepts that, it appeared increasingly, just might work.

Time out for Korea ... Chinese communists in quilted coats ... blood and iron and freezing death.

Well, at least it would pay for the rest of the doctorate, under the GI Bill.

If he lived through it.

The notice of the car crash reached him at Heartbreak Ridge.

No mother now, no father. Just an inheritance.

More courses, more digging, more Professor's letters, pulsing excitement and jubilation for all their veiled language.

Home again. Back to the university. The shock of seeing at first hand just how far The Professor had gone; how short a distance there remained to go.

And then, at last, The Girl, and the old line about passes and glasses turning out not always to be true after all.

More courses, more digging, more months slipping by. The discussions, increasingly acerbic, as it developed that The Director was a stiff-necked, belligerent bigot who classed Sir Arthur Evans and God in that order when it came to authority on matters Minoan.

The Girl, encouraging, all intellect and well-bred adoration. The Professor, designing a new-type radiation detector to help search out the truth about Knossos' fall, just in case they never did get the time inverter to work properly.

The Director, adamant.

The inverter, failing again and and again.

The faint, nagging disappointment of discovering that The Girl could discuss the courtship customs of Papua and Parthia and Patagonia in detail, yet still hold a man at arm's length here on the campus.

But still, there was his dissertation to sustain him, his long-planned trip to Crete to cling to. Even if it took every penny of his inheritance, even if The Girl wouldn't marry him and go along because he still lacked his degree, the journey couldn't help but prove worthwhile.

By air, to London. Then to Athens and the British School, to complete contacts.

Finally, down across the Aegean to Crete itself.

He had to shove his hands deep into his pockets to hide their trembling when first he stepped from the car at Knossos. Even seeing the reconstructed palace with his own eyes shook him that much.

The British, polite and helpful as they tried to hide their amusement at the use of the detector. The Cretan workmen, exchanging glances that said openly that he was surely mad.

And then, the needle, going crazy—trying to bounce clear off the dial. The headphones, buzzing till his ears hurt.

Endless hours of aching to talk to someone, yet not daring. Long days when the right words for the dissertation just wouldn't come.

And the words had to be right, exactly. He couldn't content himself with anything less. The whole dissertation—every page, every sentence, must be logic-grounded, solidly-documented, overwhelming evidence to prove his hypothesized explanation of the fall of Knossos.

He finished it, finally ... came home again ... turned in the first draft....

Then came that day in The Director's office. That ugly day, the last Burke was to spend in his own time and place.

The argument; the tempers, rising.

The Director—face flushed, jaw outthrust: "You young whelp, how dare you contradict Sir Arthur Evans? Would you set yourself up on a level with Hogarth? Pendlebury? Wace?" And then, the final knife-thrust: "Very well; have it your way. But so far as I'm concerned, I'll not accept this dissertation, now or ever. And so long as I'm here, you'll receive no doctorate, let alone a recommendation of any sort!"

Exit The Director. Forever.

Then, The Girl: "But Dion! Why did you have to be so stubborn? You could at least have kept your opinions to yourself till later. Now—well, how much of a field is there for an archaeologist with only an M. A. degree? You might as well forget Crete right now. And for my part, I must admit the idea of being the wife of an instructor in some second-rate college, at four thousand a year hardly appeals to me."

Exit The Girl. Forever.

The Research Professor, finally: "Damn it, Burke, I just don't dare to back you on it! Old Ape-Jaw's got the president's ear. If I even let it be known I designed that detector, I'll be operating this laboratory on a negative budget next biennium."

Exit The Professor. Forever.

In spirit, at least.

In body, though, he still might have his uses.

Burke held his voice carefully level. "In other words, then, you won't even let me use your name as supporting authority for my statement that the ruins at Knossos still show radiation traces?"

The Professor: "I'm sorry, Dion."

"But the time inverter—"

"Are you completely insane, boy? I built that thing with university funds. If anyone should find out about it, and that I didn't have proper authorization for it—well, all I've got to say is that I'm going to junk it first thing in the morning, before The Director has a chance to snoop around."

What happens to a man when he plunges into that deep a pit? How many blows can he take before he cracks?

Burke didn't even recognize that it was raining when he stepped out into the street.

Dully, he tramped through the gathering dusk. Block after block, mile after mile, hardly aware that his clothes clung to his body, soaked, or that water sloshed in and out of his shoes with every step.

Slowly, then, his thoughts began to sort themselves into some sort of order. A little at a time, conclusions took form and gave strength.

When it came right down to it, he didn't give a hang whether he ever achieved a Ph. D. degree or not.

So to hell with The Director!

As for security, a job, he'd lived through Heartbreak Ridge; and after that, any more economic peril came out as strictly anticlimax.

Losing The Girl—well, he had no choice but to admit it bruised his ego. Yet, on the other hand, it relieved him of all the gnawing inner doubts, the secret hesitations at her coolness.

The Professor? Another disappointment. But the mere fact that an idol's feet turned out to be of clay hardly rated as a unique discovery.

At any rate, he'd survive it.

So, what did that leave of his losses?

He cringed.

That was the way with dreams. They were so hard to give up.

And he'd worked towards this one for so long.

Now, there was nothing left to do but face the facts: he'd never have a chance at Crete; never really know for sure why Knossos fell.

Unless—

Burke stopped short.

What had The Professor said? That he'd destroy the time inverter first thing tomorrow morning?

Which still left tonight, didn't it?

It was a thought to appall any man in his right mind. For while The Professor admitted to small progress with the machine, he also said frankly that he was completely stymied in the most vital area: while he had succeeded in transporting objects from present to past on an experimental basis, he couldn't move them even an instant into the future.

Carrying this a step further, anything sent into the past stayed there. It couldn't be returned to the present.

And that meant that if anyone named Dion Burke should prove so mad as to send himself back to Bronze Age Crete, there he'd stay, with no chance ever of return to Twentieth Century United States.

It was a thought to numb a man.

Yet, was it really so insane?

After all, what was more important to him than that he learn the truth about the fall of ancient Knossos? What else could satisfy him, after all these years?

Even if he died, it wouldn't matter too much. His parents were already gone, his friends mostly on the casual side.

For the first time, now, it dawned on Burke that rain was splattering in his face. It felt good. His clothes and shoes—he didn't even care that they were ruined.

Pivoting, he started the long tramp back to his apartment.

There, for comfort, he took a hot shower; then put on a clean, dry outfit.

It seemed like a good idea, also, to check his watch, fill his cigarette lighter, and stow the old five-shot Smith & Wesson thirty-eight he'd inherited from his father in the waistband of his trousers.

By the time he'd completed all such arrangements, the rain had stopped. Here and there, stars shone amid the thin clouds overhead.

Head up, shoulders back, Burke strolled along the wet, glistening walk towards the campus. He felt somehow detached, apart from the world about him, and it was a good feeling, even though he also enjoyed the smell of the rain-soaked earth, and the way leaves had piled up in little dams along the gutter, and the hissing, whispering sound of tires on wet pavement every time a car went by. Once he even caught himself smiling a little, a small, quiet, secret smile, over the way The Director and The Girl and The Professor each in turn had looked as they took their stands and walked out of his life.

The main door of the Science Institute was still unlocked, so Burke went on in, pausing only to nod pleasantly to a campus policeman who happened to pass by at the moment.

The laboratory had a glass-paned door. Without hesitation, Burke rapped a hole in it with the butt of his revolver, reached in long enough to turn back the bolt, then stepped inside and locked the door again behind him.

Now he turned to the inner room where The Professor dealt with his most private matters.

The first thing he noted upon entering was a cluttered desk, on one corner of which lay a flat box perhaps five by eight by two inches in size.

That pleased him, for by its grilled front he recognized the thing as the incredible, transistor-packed device The Professor described as a "computational translator." Experiments with assorted foreign students and American Indians of various tribes indicated that it would enable a man to conduct a successful two-way conversation in any language.

Strapping the box in place flat against his belly, Burke moved on past the desk.

Beyond it, around a corner, loomed the time inverter.

It was a cumbersome-looking thing, a cramped platform suspended amid grids of wire. Each grid, in turn, fitted within a larger framework appropriately equipped with calibrated spindles, so that the grids' relative position to each other and to the inner platform could be adjusted at will.

To one side, a neat control-board occupied a wall-space. A larger area was given over to a screen somewhat like that of a television set.

Warily, Burke picked his way over to the screen. Now that he was here, his stomach showed a strong tendency to quiver. Despite all the long nights he'd spent in this room with The Professor, he found himself doubting his own ability to operate the inverter. As for the theory of the thing, that was completely beyond him.

But it was no time for doubt. Switching on the power, Burke carefully set about adjusting the control dials.

Latitude and longitude came first, down to minutes and then seconds. A moment's tuning, and Crete and then the Great Palace of Knossos lay before him on the scanner screen.

Falling back a step, Burke rubbed the nape of his neck where it ached from strain.

Time adjustment, now. A new set of dials.

The screen changed before his eyes. The work of excavation and reconstruction vanished. Off to one side, olive groves appeared. Then a building with unmistakably Byzantine architecture flashed on.

Again Burke twisted the dial. Again.

Now whole towns came and went. One moment, the screen showed neat huts and cultivated fields; the next, ruins or no buildings at all.

But never a trace of people. People moved too quickly for even the finest settings of the time-spindles to show them.

Farther back ... farther ... farther....

And now there was only a great, dark ring on the hillside to mark the palace. Wall-blocks and pillars lay strewn like scorched blocks in all directions. It was as if lightning had blasted the very earth. The few huts to be seen stood far off, as if the site of Knossos were a place accursed, to be avoided under pain of death.

A chill touched Burke; and though he'd seen this sight a dozen times before, his fingers trembled.

Back farther ... farther....

As swiftly as it had darkened, the screen came bright. The palace rose again, white gypsum walls and columns aglisten in the sunlight.

Skillfully, Burke adjusted the detail dial, working forward again to the moment when the palace had crumbled.

The disaster came at night; that was plain to see. And so fast that the screen could not record the instant when it happened. One second, the buildings were there, solid as only rock could make them.

The next, there were only dark, blighted ruins.

Of course, the destruction could conceivably have taken hours, yet still show as instantaneous on the scanner.

But if a man were to go back to a time, say, twelve hours before the cataclysm....

He'd need to choose the right place, too ... somewhere out of the line of palace traffic—that apartment off the Queen's Megaron, for instance.

Not too steadily, Burke set the dials; then straightened.

The realization of his own folly flooded through him in the same instant.

How could anyone be so mad as to sacrifice his life on the altar of sheer intellectual curiosity? What did it matter if he never knew why Knossos fell? To go through with this because he'd been intrigued by an octopus-decorated Minoan bowl as a child of seven—it was absurd. His place was here—in his own time, his own land. To think otherwise could only be evidence of gross imbalance.

He started to reach for the main switch; to turn off the inverter.

Simultaneously, a hand rattled the knob of the laboratory's outer door.

Burke froze.

Now a key clicked in the lock. A voice—the voice of the campus policeman—called, "All right, you! Come on out! We know you're there!"

And then, not quite so plainly, the voice of The Professor: "Be careful, officer. He's been acting queerly—thinks I've some kind of strange machine in there. What he needs is a psychiatrist. But till we can get him to one, he may be dangerous."

The Professor, coppering his bets ... taking no chances on trouble over having misused university funds to finance a private project.

Not even if it involved proclaiming a friend insane.

The final straw, piled on the camel's back.

And only one way out.

Savagely, Burke whipped the Smith & Wesson from his belt; then, tight-lipped, flicked a quick glance along the dials.

The inverter was as ready as it ever would be.

Breathing hard, Burke slid between the wire grids; stepped up onto the cramped central platform.

From the outer room: "Come out, now, Burke! You'll have a chance to prove you're sane—just a few tests, a month or two of observation—"

Burke gripped the activating switch, the lever that would throw full power into the grids.

Again, then, he hesitated.

The campus policeman's head appeared around the corner, peering. To one side, The Professor cried out. "The inverter—! Stop him!"

It was like a wire snapping in Burke's brain. He fired a single shot, high, and simultaneously threw the activating switch in one swift, coordinated flow of motion.

The grid-wires glowed. A tingle of energy pulsed through Burke's body.

The laboratory disappeared....

CHAPTER IV

Burke heard the voices first—strange voices, speaking in a strange language.

The room came clear a moment later, cool and shadowy. Burke recognized it by its shape, and by the distinctive relief in painted stucco on one wall.

So his calculations had been correct. He'd landed in the apartment off the Queen's Megaron.

Cat-like, he moved towards the room's doorway, the voices.

The speakers were man and woman, apparently. And when Burke flicked the switch of the computational translator strapped tight to his belly, he found he could understand them almost as well as if they'd been talking English.

"... and you're a pretty thing, you know," the man was saying. "As a matter of fact...."

His voice trailed off, the last words lost in a rising feminine giggle. "Master Theseus! You're here to see my mistress, not me—"

Warily, Burke peered through the grating of a sort of grilled divider that helped to separate room from room.

The chamber beyond was larger than the one in which he stood. Brighter, too—a typical Minoan light-well spilled noonday sun clear along one side. The furnishings and the octopus frescoes on the wall showed an opulence that spoke of nothing less than royalty.

As for the man and the woman, they were alone in the room, and playing a game as old as time. That is, the man was trying to catch the woman—girl, really—while she strove to stay out of his reach.

Burke decided he could have taken her efforts more seriously if she hadn't kept giggling—not to mention slowing whenever the man gave any sign of pausing in his pursuit.

Then, abruptly, the man leaped across a low table, cutting her off.

The girl promptly tripped, and fell into his arms.

The embrace that followed was a trifle too prolonged for Burke's tastes. When it ended, the girl sighed, starry-eyed, and ran long, supple fingers through her companion's short black hair. "How can a warrior such as you, a hero, even look at a serving-wench like me, Master Theseus?" she murmured.

The man straightened and swelled out his chest; and now Burke saw that he was not only a good six feet tall and powerfully built, but handsome in a somewhat coarse, heavy-featured way.

"I'll deny no wench my favors just because she's of a lower station," he proclaimed pompously. "I've no doubt you'll keep a man as warm as this Princess Ariadne who's your mistress."

The girl giggled. "You mustn't say such things, Master Theseus! Ariadne's the loveliest woman in all Knossos."

"What—?" Theseus' broad brow furrowed, and he stood with mouth half open, looking more than a little stupid. "Are you trying to confuse me, wench? If this Ariadne's such a beauty, why must she send secretly for prisoners from her father's dungeon in order to find lovers?"

An uneasy shadow seemed to fall across the maid's pretty face. She moved restlessly. "It—it's the curse of Pasiphae, Master Theseus."

"The curse of Pasiphae—?" Theseus looked blank. "What's that, wench? Tell me of it."

"Of the curse?" The girl's smile grew suddenly stiff, and her hands moved in a small, nervous gesture.

Then, quickly, she came close to her barrel-chested companion and slipped her arms about him. "No wonder you're the pride of Athens, Master Theseus! Close to you this way, I feel your strength. It brings a woman all sorts of thoughts—"

Belligerently, Theseus scowled and pushed her back. "None of that, wench! This curse—tell me about it!"

The girl drew a deep, unhappy breath, "If you must, then—" And, after a moment's pause: "You know, of course, that Pasiphae is King Minos' wife; Ariadne's mother?"

"Yes."

"And also that she lusted after the sacred bull of Zeus—"

"—and so gave birth to the monster in the Labyrinth, the Minotaur? Of course. Who hasn't heard it?"

The maid looked round almost fearfully. "Do you not see, then, Master Theseus? There's the curse! Ariadne's daughter of a woman who's defied all the laws of gods and men. Who knows what evil may befall the child? So, no youth dares even look at Ariadne, no matter how great her beauty."

Theseus' jaw sagged for a moment. Then he bristled. "It's not because of my fame, then, my prowess as a lover, that she sent you to bring me here in secret?"

The maid bowed her head. But from his vantage-point, Burke could see her hidden smile—quick, minx-like. "She seeks only to escape her destiny, Master Theseus. In you, hero that you are, she sees one who might slay the Minotaur and take her away from Crete and the scorn and loneliness that so long have been her lot here."

"So!" grunted Theseus. "She'd use me, would she! Me, hero of Athens!"

His scowl grew even blacker. Then, abruptly, it faded. Sweeping the girl up bodily in his arms, he bore her to the nearest couch. "Enough of this empty talk, wench! We've wasted too much time already on your precious mistress!"

The couch groaned with their joint weight. Throwing the maid back, tilting her face up, Theseus strove to kiss her.

But now the girl drew away, struggling in obvious earnest. "No, Master Theseus, no! We dare not! Ariadne may come at any moment—"

"Let her come!" Athenian pinned maid with hands and body. "Let her see for herself who I prefer—"

Across the room, a door opened. A slim young girl, proud-faced and beautiful and poised, stood framed within the entry.

On the couch, the maid gave a little shriek. "Princess Ariadne!" Frantically, she tried to writhe free of Theseus.

He clutched at her as she spun erect. Cloth ripped as her whole skirt tore away, leaving her standing well-nigh naked.

The maid's face flamed. Whirling, she darted for the grill-masked doorway where Burke stood hiding.

It took him off balance; it was that unexpected. Before he could even get clear, jump back, she dodged behind the grating; crashed into him full-tilt.

Burke reeled back against the door-frame.

The maid screamed.

Like an echo, Theseus tore away the screening grillwork.

After that, for Burke, there was no choice. Instinctively, he knew that no matter what the cost, he must gain command of the situation.

Snatching the Smith & Wesson from his waistband, he leveled it at Theseus. "Stand back, you!"

Apparently the computational translator put words and tone into language the bull-necked Athenian could understand. He stopped short.

Catching the maid by the shoulder, Burke shoved her, stumbling, over to join her playmate.

Next, Ariadne, still standing frozen beside the far door:

"You, princess!" Burke clipped tightly. "Over here, on the double!"

The slim girl didn't move a muscle.

Burke snapped, "Come here, I said! Now! Do you hear me?"

Coldly, the great dark eyes took in Burke and his so-different garments. Then, in a voice edged with scorn, the princess asked, "And who are you, to command the daughter of Minos in her own chambers?"

Sweat slicked Burke's palms, his forehead. "That doesn't matter. It's enough that I hold the power of the thunderbolt in my hand here." He gestured with the Smith & Wesson.

"Indeed?" Now, coolly, Ariadne strolled in his direction. "Perhaps, then, you're a god; is that it?"

Burke groped. "Perhaps."

"Or more likely, you're just a thief from some far country." The girl stood very erect before Burke, oval face even lovelier for her anger. "What brought you to my chambers, dog? Or must I have you flayed alive to get an answer?"

The trouble with taking command of a situation, Burke decided, was that you had to be willing to go all out. And he wasn't.

At least, not with this slim young beauty.

Desperately, he tried a final gambit. "You, Theseus! Seize her!"

But now the Athenian's eyes had narrowed. His head came forward, just a fraction. It had the effect of making his body loom even larger than before. He looked belligerent and dangerous.

Burke tried again. "Theseus—"

"No."

Without volition, Burke found his finger tightening on the Smith & Wesson's trigger.

Beside Theseus, the maid whimpered. "Master Theseus—the thunderbolts—"

The Athenian snorted. "He's no god; he's a man. But if he reaches Minos with a tale of having found me in the Princess Ariadne's quarters, I'll be a long time dying." He licked thick lips. "No. Better that *he* should die. Here. Now."

He lunged at Burke.

Leaping aside, Burke thrust a foot between his charging adversary's legs.

The Athenian lurched wildly, clawing at the air.

Gun high for a quick blow, Burke leaped in close behind him.

Only then, incredibly, the other was whirling on one foot, with all the grace and skill of a ballet dancer.

Simultaneously, the other foot whipped up, kicking for Burke's groin.

With a desperate effort, Burke caught the blow on his forearms.

But now it was he who'd been feinted off balance. Before he could recover, a left-handed blow sent him tottering backwards.

Then he hit a couch. His knees hinged. He sprawled belly-up exposed and helpless.

Like lightning, Theseus seized a great stone jar, a pithoi. Muscles bulging, with unbelievable strength he swung it high above his head, poised to dash down on Burke.

Burke jerked his revolver up and fired in one spasmodic movement, straight at the pithoi.

Gun-thunder echoed through the chamber. The great jar shattered, cascading slack-jawed Theseus with shards and oil.

Burke rolled from the couch and stumbled to a new defense-point against the nearest wall.

But one shot had been enough for the Hero of Athens. He still stood blank-eyed, looking more stupid than ever as he stared in a sort of numb fascination at the shattered stoneware about his feet.

As for the maid, she'd fainted. And the expression lovely Ariadne now wore was beyond Burke's power to read.

But already, feet were pounding in the corridor outside. Guards poured into the room, half-a-dozen of them—great, strapping blacks with spears and swords and shields.

Six guards ... and only three shots left in the revolver.

Now the Cretan who seemed to be in command of the Negroes looked about uncertainly. "What happened, princess?" he asked. "Who are these men, these strangers?"

For a moment, Burke thought, a smile almost flickered at the corners of Ariadne's mouth.

Then, coolly, she said, "They're strangers to me, too, warrior. I only know that when I came in, this one"—a gesture to Burke—"was tearing the clothes from my maid. Then, he swore he'd possess me, also, and would have, had it not been that this other,"—the gesture was to Theseus this time—"fought to save me."

The Cretan's nostrils flared. He spat an order to the guards: "This dog is yours. Slay him!"

Burke's stomach churned. It was all he could do to breathe.

Was this the way his dream must end—here, now, before he'd even learned the secret he'd come after?

Only then, as the blacks started forward, Ariadne spoke again: "No, guards! Don't kill him!" And slowly, calculatingly, dark eyes strangely brooding: "For this man says he's a god, and for such a blasphemer a quick death is too good.

"So, let him live—to face my father, Minos!"

CHAPTER V

The place was called the Shrine of Oracles, Burke gathered. It featured distinctively Minoan pillars—of cypress, and so tapered as to be smaller at the base than at the top.

Also, it stank with a peculiar, acrid odor.

But beyond that, to Burke, it seemed disappointingly ordinary ... hardly colorful enough to rate the trial of a man accused of playing god.

That is, so it appeared until his captors dragged him into a central room ... and there, black-browed and haughty, sat bearded Minos on his throne.

A chill ran through Burke. Never had he seen such malevolence staring out of human eyes.

For his own part, it would be the supreme test of his skill and daring if he even left this room alive. With all his heart, he wished he had the Smith & Wesson back.

Lacking it, he'd have to rely upon his wits and play the scene by ear.

And that brought up another nagging question: why had Ariadne insisted on possessing herself of the weapon? And why did she take such pains to stay well separated from him, with others of his captors always in between?

Studying her now, it once again came home to Burke that she was indeed a strange, a tragic figure, for all her loveliness. For even here, in the presence of the mighty sea-king who was her father, her isolation showed up all too clearly. The guards, the priests, the nobles—as one, they walked wide around her, as if some mark of shame and menace were blazoned on her forehead.

Perhaps—

But now Minos leaned forward upon his carved gypsum throne. "Well, blasphemer? How do you choose to die?"

The monarch's voice echoed the black hatred of all mankind that gleamed with such intensity in his eyes.

Burke forced himself to boldness. "Who says I blaspheme?" he demanded.

"Do you deny it, then, dog?" King Minos came up from his throne in blazing fury. "Do you dare to say that the Princess Ariadne, my own daughter, lies?"

"When she says I claim to be a god? No." Burke laughed harshly. And then, with sudden inspiration: "It's only the blasphemy I deny; not the godhood."

"Not the godhood—?" Now Minos' eyes distended. A note of uncertainty crept into his voice. "You mean, you stand before me claiming kinship to the mighty ones, the lords of earth and sea and sky who rule men's destinies?"

"Do you doubt it?"

"Then name yourself, mocker! Who is it you claim to be?"

With a strange sort of detachment, Burke found himself mentally flicking through the pantheon for some name that would fit well with his own.

"Well, blasphemer?"

Burke twisted his mouth into a thin, wry smile. "Would you disown mighty Dionysus?" he queried coolly. "Would you drive from your midst the giver of grapes and wine and joy?"

"Dionysus—!" In awed whispers, the name ran round the crowded room.

For the fraction of a second, Minos' gaze flickered.

Only then, a new storm of belligerence seemed to shake him. He strode forward, shaking his fist. "We'll see, dog! We'll see! The oracle shall decide!"

The whole throne-room quivered with sudden hushed fear.

"Make way!" roared Minos. "Make way to the shrine, that the oracle himself may judge this mocker!"

Then, to Burke: "—And if he declares you false, you dog, you'll wish I'd thrown you to the Minotaur before you die!"

He pivoted; stalked down an aisle formed by the onlookers.

Roughly, Burke's guards shoved him along behind. A stone-walled well loomed, with broad steps leading down.

—The lustral area! The sacred place of purification that Sir Arthur Evans first had assumed to be a bath!

Only now, it was turning out in reality to be for revelation, not purification; a holy of holies where Man could receive the pronouncements of the gods.

The guards let go of Burke when he reached the steps. Apparently they had no intention of following him down into the pit itself.

Of a sudden he felt strangely nervous. His knees showed a tendency to shake.

But he couldn't let that happen, and he knew it. Not if he wanted ever to leave this weird place alive. So he straightened his shoulders and clenched his teeth and strode boldly after King Minos.

With every step, the biting, acrid smell grew stronger. Burke almost choked on it. He found himself wondering if perhaps the oracle spoke in trances induced by vapors; if maybe this pit were outlet for a pocket of some sort of natural gas.

Not even a whisper rose from the watchers in the throne-room. The only sound was the scrape of his own shoes upon the stone.

Then, at last, he and Minos reached the bottom of the stair. Dramatically, the sea-king threw wide his arms. "Mighty oracle of Zeus, it is your chosen one who calls!" he thundered. "Speak to me! Tell me—tell all of us—if this creature here beside me is a god!"

Silence.

"Speak, oracle! Give us your answer! Is this truly Dionysus? Or is it but a man, a blasphemer we should slay?"

More silence.

Burke choked on a sudden impulse to laugh. To think of it—a twentieth century man and a Bronze Age sea-king, together in this dank, smelly hole, calling on the gods for a revelation!

And what if the oracle's secret really turned out to be gas? Might it prove his own salvation—or at least give him a quick and easy death?

For instance, suppose he were to flick the wheel of his pocket lighter—would the all-pervasive smell explode or burn?

"Oracle, I am your chosen one, King Minos! I command you—"

Quietly, Burke palmed the lighter.

"Speak, oracle; speak!"

A sudden recklessness surged through Burke. He opened his mouth to laugh.

And stopped stone cold.

Because suddenly, out of nowhere, another mind was probing in his brain!

Instinctively, he strove to force out the invader.

The very effort gave him new insight. For now, as he fought, he knew that the mind which he had joined in combat was not human, but alien. Its whole quality and mode of thought were of another order, another realm.

Feeling that mind, fighting it, Burke all at once understood the malevolence he'd seen in Minos' eyes.

In the sea-king, he faced a man possessed.

Now, the alien thing sought to possess him, too.

Savagely, Burke met its probings. Sweating, straining, he fought it, hate for hate, and turned it back, and drove it from his brain.

Then, as quickly as it had come, the pressure was gone.

But in the same instant, Minos cried out, "This is no god! This is but a man!"

And from the crowd above, a thunderous echo: "Yes, yes! He's but a man!"

The bearded king turned on Burke. His sword-point scraped the grillwork of the translator case still strapped flat against Burke's belly beneath the clothes. "Up, dog! Up from this holy shrine and meet your doom!"

Bleak, dry-lipped, Burke started up the stair.

At the top, directly ahead of him and in the front row of those waiting, stood Ariadne.

As he climbed, now, her eyes caught his and, burning, held them for a moment. Then her hands moved in a quick, restricted gesture that momentarily pulled her stylized apron to one side.

The Smith & Wesson hung beneath it.

Burke drew a shallow, unsteady breath.

Six steps more and he'd be at floor level. That left no time to question motives.

Casually, he flipped back his lighter's lid.

Three steps more, now.

Another quick, shallow breath. Then, spinning the lighter's wheel with his right thumb, he knocked Minos' sword from his back with his left forearm and thrust flame straight at the sea-king's eyes.

The monarch gave a choked, incoherent yell and jerked back. A shove, and he was crashing down the stair.

Whirling, Burke charged like a battering-ram straight into the crowd at the head of the steps.

Screams, scrambling, panic. Burke dived across two fallen priests, at Ariadne.

The next instant he had the revolver, and his free arm was locked about her waist. When a thick-shouldered noble started towards him, swinging a great double-axe, he fired by sheer reflex.

The axeman stopped short, a shocked expression on his face and a hole in his chest. When he fell, the whole throne-room sounded with the hiss of breaths sharply indrawn.

Burke rapped, "I'm leaving. Your princess goes with me. Try to stop me and she dies!"

Out the door, then. Down a corridor.

Ariadne whispered, "Quick, my lord Dionysus! Up this stair, here!"

More halls, more stairways. Big rooms and little.

Finally, a tiny, windowless cubicle opening off a light-well.

———————————————

Burke turned to Ariadne. "All right, princess. We'll hide here till dark, then get you out of Knossos."

A look of strain came to the girl's face. "My lord, it—it cannot be."

"It can't?"

"No, my lord. We—I—I dare not leave the palace. My father's men— they'd run me down within a finger's-breadth of time."

"Oh?" Burke studied her. "Tell me, princess, what makes you so sure?"

"It—it is the Minotaur, my brother." Ariadne's face took on a heightened color. "You see, Lord Dionysus, at my father's will the monster holds me here within the palace. No matter how I try to hide or run away, always he tracks me down."

Burke stood very still. "He—tracks you down—?"

"Yes, my lord." The girl raised a restless hand to smooth her jet-black hair. "His mind—it follows mine, you see. So when I would flee, he sends pursuers to drag me back." And then: "Lord Dion, I confess: at first I sought to save you so that you, a god, would slay the Minotaur and carry me away."

"I see."

"But now—I'm not so sure that you're a god."

"So?"

"So ... so...." The girl's voice broke. She hid her face. "My lord, I know only that I bear a curse. So, you must go quickly, and forget me. Because if you should die on my account, I—I—"

Her words faded into sobs.

A sudden tenderness rose in Burke. He held the shaking girl close.

And then, all at once, the things he felt were beyond tenderness.

It gave his problem a new dimension; added another element to complicate his road.

"Could it be that the Minotaur and the oracle really are one?" he asked abruptly.

Ariadne lifted a tear-stained face. "How did you guess, my lord?"

"This mind-track business—do you have any idea how it works?"

The girl's cheeks flamed. "Don't shame me, Lord Dionysus! You know he's only—half—my brother."

"And on account of that wild story about the sacred bull and your mother, Pasiphae, you think he's got powers beyond the human?" Burke snorted. "Believe me, princess, it isn't true. Either that creature's not half a bull, or else he's not half your brother. A thing called science says it can't be." He grinned suddenly. "My own bet's that he's neither bull nor human. And maybe the best way to check on that is to ask your mother a few questions."

"Then I'll come with you!" This eagerly, from Ariadne.

Burke shook his head. "No. We'll not risk your pretty neck on the kind of thing I need to do."

"To walk with a god can bring no risk, my lord."

"That's just the trouble, princess," Burke acknowledged ruefully. "You see, you were right. I'm a man, not a god."

"Then all the more reason for me to stay with you."

"There's no use arguing. It's settled."

A small foot, stamping. "Lord Dion, I shall go!"

"Sorry, princess." Burke smiled bleakly. "I'll see you at your quarters later. Meanwhile...."

He struck quick and hard, straight to her jaw, then gently stretched her limp form on the floor....

CHAPTER VI

It was a jigsaw puzzle with too many pieces, Burke decided. No matter how he tried to analyze it, he always came out with a vital fragment or two left over.

Take the Minotaur. Did such a creature actually exist? Or was the thing simply a figment of imagination?

Assuming its existence, what about the strange mental powers with which it had tried to probe his brain?

Alien powers.

Yet if it were alien, what was King Minos' relation to it? Why would a human join hands with anything that radiated such malevolence and hate?

Or, for that matter, what was the relation between the sea-king and his own daughter, Ariadne? Freudians would have a field day with that business of the mind-thing's holding her within the palace at her father's behest.

Finally, staying on the personal level, where did Pasiphae fit in? What lay behind the legend of her having bribed Daedalus the Smith to build her a wooden cow so that she could be joined with the sacred bull? Could she actually have given birth to the Minotaur, or was that tale merely symbolic?

Then, looking at the larger elements, the questions that had brought him here to start with, what was the origin of the radiation traces on the site of Knossos? And how had the city so mysteriously fallen in a single night?

Questions without answers, so far. All of them.

Further—Burke checked his watch—it was past four now, and that meant he had only eight hours more before the palace met its doom.

Yet he couldn't take Ariadne out till he'd somehow immobilized the Minotaur.

Cursing under his breath, he wondered what had become of Pasiphae; why she wasn't where she belonged, in the Queen's Megaron.

Now two maids appeared, an older woman between them. Hastily, Burke flattened himself on the high ledge where he was hiding and waited to see what would happen.

Leading the woman to one of the low benches along the wall, the maids spread a tapestry-like cloth for their charge to sit upon, then withdrew. The door closed behind them.

Burke frowned. There was a strangeness about the whole procedure that puzzled him. Not a word had been spoken. And, once seated, the woman hadn't moved.

Warily, he moved a fraction closer to the edge of his ledge, so that he could see the woman better.

She was richly dressed, with skirts that fell in bright folds ornamented with lotus-blossom designs. Her bodice was the most ornate that Burke had seen.

Yet it was her face, rather than her garments, that held the largest part of Burke's attention. That this was Pasiphae, he could have no doubt. The resemblance between her and Ariadne was that marked.

The points of difference puzzled him, though. He tried to analyze them.

And then, all at once, he knew.

For where Ariadne's face was alive and expressive and animated, this woman's features sagged passive and loose. Her greying hair had the neatness of the maids' attention, but none of the flair that bespoke personal interest. Her eyes stared out vacuous and blank upon the room.

Burke's frown deepened. Carefully, he checked every detail again and again.

And then, in the position of her hands, he found the key.

For the fingers of the left were turned up and twisted at an awkward angle ... yet still they stayed there, minute after minute after minute.

Burke sucked in air. "Catatonic!" he exclaimed aloud.

The woman gave no indication that she'd heard him.

Dropping from the ledge, he came close to her: passed his hand before her eyes.

Still she gave no sign of awareness.

Burke shivered. "Pasiphae ..." he whispered. "Pasiphae!"

No answer.

Burke tried again: "Pasiphae, tell me about your son, the Minotaur."

Nothing.

"About Minos, Pasiphae. About Ariadne."

Blank, staring eyes.

Burke paused, considered. Then, leaning close, he whispered, "The thing, Pasiphae; the mind-thing. The creature that comes into your brain—"

Without warning, Pasiphae screamed. Then, before Burke could stop her, she was on her feet and darting past him—fleeing like a woman possessed down a long corridor.

Burke raced after her.

Then, just when he thought that he would catch her, she came up short; whirled on him, eyes suddenly wild and wide. "You! Are you one of them?"

"One of them—?"

"No, you're not! You don't make my head hurt like they did! They always hurt. Always ... always...."

She sagged back against the wall. Once again, her eyes began to glaze.

Burke said, "Minos, your husband ... is Minos one of them?"

Startlement. "Don't take him! Don't take my baby! I won't let them have him! I'll get him back! I will—"

The woman struck out at Burke, then ran.

Sickness in him, he followed.

Only this time, she turned sharply; plunged down a narrow flight of stairs.

Cursing, Burke half-fell down the steps.

It was dark at the bottom. He could see nothing of Pasiphae. But her footsteps still sounded so, groping, he tried to follow.

The next instant he stepped off into hip-deep water. Floundering, he fought for balance.

Something clutched at his legs.

Burke bellowed aloud from sheer shock. Desperately, he tried to scramble out of the pool.

The thing holding him let go. Shaking, Burke dragged himself onto the footwalk, flicked on his lighter, and stared down into the water.

An octopus with a head nearly double the size of his own met his gaze coldly.

Shivering, Burke closed the lighter and felt his way, an uneasy step at a time, along the edge of the tank.

Then at last he met a blank wall ... found another flight of stairs ... groped his way down them.

Close at hand, Pasiphae screamed shrilly and ran on again.

Abruptly, then, light, as a distant door opened. Burke sprinted towards it.

Beyond, when he reached the entry, lay the strangest room he'd ever seen.

For this was no half-barbaric Bronze Age chamber. Instead, it shimmered with the cold fire of a blue-white metal the like of which Burke had never seen before. Light pulsed from it—all of it, till he felt as if he were walking in some sort of tremendous lamp.

And there ahead, at the far end of the room, was Pasiphae.

Again, Burke sprinted.

Laughing wildly, the woman stepped into a cubicle.

Like magic, she vanished.

For an instant Burke hesitated, then entered the box-like area himself.

This time, the room through which he'd come vanished.

Almost instantly, then, another chamber appeared—one so vast Burke couldn't be sure where it ended.

A thing like a flattened cone stood in the chamber's center, looming like a miniature mountain.

Or perhaps one not so miniature.

It, too, was of the shimmering, blue-white metal. Not a sign of an opening marred its shining surface.

And yet, Burke realized numbly, there must be ports of some sort.

Because the thing was beyond all doubt a space-ship, a vessel designed for interplanetary—maybe even interstellar—travel.

It came to Burke in that moment, with grim humor, that he'd found the answer to his questions; most of them, at any rate.

The radiation; Knossos' downfall; the mind-thing that was the Minotaur, or vice versa—all such came clear now.

This was an alien colony, set down on Crete. Which meant that anything which might befall the native population would, in the eyes of the invaders, be seen as no great issue.

So, this was a good place to be away from; and the quicker, the better.

Bleakly, he looked around for Pasiphae.

She stood cowering a dozen yards away, eyes fixed blankly on the gigantic alien craft.

Slowly, carefully, Burke approached her. The best idea he could think of was to take her hand; he'd read somewhere that leading was the best procedure in dealing with any mental case.

Gently, he reached out.

But when his fingers touched hers, it was as if an electric shock had leaped between them. Screaming as before, Pasiphae ran from him.

From him, and straight towards the space-ship.

In frantic haste, Burke started to follow.

Only then, all at once, there was a blinding flash that centered on the woman. Tendrils of smoke curled up from a charred, crumbling husk.

Sick with horror, Burke stared for one brief moment. Then, at the double, he hurried back to the cubicle from which he'd stepped.

Now he noted that a duplicate stood beside it. Which, he assumed, meant that this was a two-way transportation system, leading from the ship to Knossos. How far apart the two were, he couldn't even guess at. Miles, probably. The very fact that transportation was called for would indicate that.

He stepped into the second cubicle; then, a moment later, out again in the room beneath the palace.

It bothered him a little that he still hadn't seen any of the aliens. He liked the idea of knowing what he was fighting.

But that couldn't be helped. The important thing now was to act quickly; to meet and defeat the Minotaur so that he could get Ariadne out of the palace before it was destroyed.

He checked his watch: nearly eight already. It was incredible how fast time slipped away.

Back up the stairs and through the tank-room to the Queen's Megaron. Then out the light-well by which he'd entered, and through the gathering dark to the Shrine of Oracles.

Because that was where he'd have to start; he knew that from the things he'd heard as prisoner. The entrance to the Labyrinth, the way to the Minotaur, was through some passage in the shrine.

Only there was a guard on the first entrance he tried, and on the second also.

In ten minutes he knew the truth: a mouse couldn't creep into the shrine tonight without being run through by a Sudani spearman.

So, he had no choice but to try a different route, the route of legend.

First, he'd have to locate Ariadne, even though it demanded another hair-raising human fly act, clambering down a pitch-black light-well.

Then, through her, he'd reach Daedalus, demand a thread, plunge into the Labyrinth.

Only that wasn't right. The legend said Theseus did that.

Yet Theseus was drunk, dead drunk, back there in Ariadne's quarters.

Or was he?

It dawned on Burke, then, that nothing but delirium could account for such confusion. How else could he be flying and falling at once? What other explanation would take in such a strange, shifting mixture of past and present?

Then, suddenly, he became aware of the cold stone beneath his back. In a flash, he remembered how Theseus had trapped him ... forced him into the sewer ... dragged him to the Labyrinth's one secret entrance ... struck him down....

CHAPTER VII

Consciousness returned to Burke with dragging steps.

Perhaps that was because the place in which he now lay was so dark. It stayed that way even when his bruised jaw and aching head told him for certain that this was reality, not delusion. No matter how he strained his eyes, he could see absolutely nothing.

Not that it mattered. Because he knew where he was, beyond mistaking. His nose told him, picking up the acrid scent that had been so all-pervasive in the Shrine of Oracles.

Only here, it was worse. Here, it rose sharp and biting as the very smell of death.

And that meant he could be nowhere but in the Labyrinth itself!

The thought knotted Burke's stomach. Yet when he strove to move, his bonds held him, unyielding.

Theseus had done this job well, Burke decided. With no trouble at all, it could spell doom for him.

Which brought up another question: what time was it?

By the very fact that he remained alive, he assumed it still wasn't midnight; that Knossos hadn't been destroyed.

But even if he'd blacked out only for two or three minutes, the fatal moment couldn't be far off ... not more than half an hour, at most.

It was the kind of thought to put a man upon his mettle. Floundering, Burke tried to break his bonds.

It was useless. The cords wouldn't give a fraction.

That meant he had to find some other way out.

Twisting, he made an effort to check his pockets' contents.

Small change, a comb, two keys, his lighter.

His lighter—!

Involuntarily, Burke breathed faster. Squirming, writhing, he strained to bring his bound hands to where one could reach into the proper pocket, instead of just feeling what was there through fabric.

Now tingling fingers told him the cords had cut off circulation. Let his hands get too numb, and he wouldn't even be able to hold the lighter.

A final effort. One thumb slipped into the pocket. Burke hooked it into the opening and heaved.

A seam ripped, noisy in the stillness. The pocket's contents rattled on the stone floor.

Rolling over again, Burke groped till his trembling fingers found the lighter. Flicking back the lid, he spun the wheel.

Flame licked at the palm of his other hand. For a moment it was all he could do to keep from crying out, dropping the lighter.

But he gritted his teeth instead and, sweat streaming down his face, forced himself to lower the lighter carefully so that it stood upright on the floor.

Now, once again, speed became the issue. It went without saying that the lighter's fluid must be almost exhausted.

If it burned out too soon—!

Burke bit down harder. Heedless of the pain and sweat and knotting muscles, he forced himself to thrust his wrists down so the flame could play upon the cords.

In seconds, the stench of searing flesh and burned cloth blotted out the chamber's odor. Eyes squeezed tight shut as if to shut out the agony, cursing beneath his breath, Burke strained to keep his bonds taut and in the right position.

Then, when it seemed that he could stand the pain no longer, a cord snapped like a clipped wire. Another followed.

The next instant, Burke's wrists were free.

Sobbing soundlessly, he batted out the lighter, to save what fuel remained.

After that, the job became routine—a matter of stripping loose ends of cord from his wrists; working his fingers till circulation was restored; untying his ankles.

The burns still hurt; and, he knew the pain would be even worse later on. What to do about it, though—that was something else again.

In any case, he needed light.

Rising, once more he flicked on the lighter.

Mostly, it revealed emptiness and shadow. But there was a lamp-stand over to one side, so Burke made his way to it and lighted the lamp.

Now, for the first time, he checked his watch.

Eleven thirty five. Less than half an hour till Knossos met its doom.

It raised a new problem: what was his own best course now? To stay here? To go seek out the Minotaur as first planned? Or to drop back through the open manhole he now spotted over in one corner, and put his trust in flight?

That last idea—it had much to commend it. For one thing, almost any manhole where he might come up, save only this one, would put him in a position to keep a whole skin and escape the palace, even without the thread of Daedalus to guide him.

For another, any attempt on his part now to slay the Minotaur was doomed to failure in advance. Obviously. Theseus had made off with the Smith & Wesson. Without it, or equivalent, no one could hope to meet the monster and live.

Lamp in hand, Burke went over to the manhole and sat down on the edge, legs dangling, in preparation for the drop into the drainage tunnel below.

Only then, as he momentarily hesitated there, bracing himself, his mind turned to the one subject he most wished to avoid.

Ariadne.

It had to come, of course. He'd known it all along. You couldn't ignore a woman in a moment of crisis such as this one—not when she meant as much to you as Ariadne did to him.

So, what would happen to her, if he dropped down through this manhole into the sewer?

Answer: she'd die. In less than half an hour she'd die, without note, in the destruction of this strange, gleaming palace men called Knossos.

And nothing he, Dion Burke, or anyone else, could do would save her, so long as the Minotaur lived.

Now the question became, did he care about escaping, living, if he had to do it alone, without his lovely Ariadne?

Burke forced himself to hesitate on that one. He didn't want to react to it hastily, or casually, or emotionally, or without due thought and consideration.

The only difficulty was, a man's feelings weren't something he could put on or take off at will, like a suit of clothes. They were part of him, incorporated into every cell of meat and blood and bone and tissue.

And there was the answer to his basic question: win or lose, live or die, he'd leave Knossos only with Ariadne at his side.

Beside, hadn't the legends said that Theseus slew the Minotaur with his bare fists? Maybe a proxy could do likewise!

Swinging his legs up out of the manhole, Burke scrambled to his feet, somewhat heavily. The burns on his wrists were hurting worse now, and he hardly felt in the best of shape to do battle with a monster.

But it seemed he had little choice. So, lamp in hand, he moved along the wall looking for an exit.

It wasn't till he'd worked his way through half-a-dozen pitch-black chambers that two things dawned on him:

First, the solution to the problem of his scorched, seared wrists was oil; and such was available in the jars that flanked almost every lamp-stand.

Second, the quickest way to the Minotaur was to follow his nose. Once he'd located the source of the strange, acrid smell, odds were he'd also have found the monster.

Doused liberally with oil, Burke's wrists felt better. And it was no feat at all to choose his path by odor.

Yet time still seeped away ... he had a bare fifteen minutes left now, if his watch and calculations proved right.

How big could this cursed maze be?

Too big, apparently.

Then, just when despair was about to overtake him, a thin line of light gleamed far ahead.

A sheen of cold sweat came to Burke's palms. He moved forward more warily, more silently, than ever.

The light, it developed, shone from the crack beneath a door.

Like a shadow, Burke crept close; laid his ear against the panel, listening.

No sound.

Ever so gently, he laid the fingers of his left hand against the portal; pressed slowly.

New light appeared, washing through the crack along the jamb.

A moment of taut waiting. Then Burke put his eye to the opening and peered through, into a large, sumptuously-furnished room. The room of a noble, perhaps, or even a king.

The only thing strange about it that Burke could see was that what appeared to be a large tank occupied the center of the room ... a tank of shimmering, blue-white metal, utterly unlike the bronze of the Minoans; precisely the same as the material of which the great ship in the cave was made.

The hair along the back of Burke's neck prickled. Moving first to one side and then the other, he checked as large a portion of the room beyond the door as possible.

No occupants, so far as he could see.

With a quick push, he sent the door all the way back, swinging wide, while he poised rigid in the shadows.

Still no reaction.

Silently, Burke crossed the threshold.

Here the acrid smell was almost overpowering; and though the room itself was unoccupied, a strange, pulsating aura of evil seemed to flow through it in great waves.

Burke tip-toed to the shining, blue-white tank; peered down into it.

It held clear liquid only. But the stink of the stuff made Burke choke and gasp. His eyes burned. He stumbled backward, fighting for breath.

In the same instant, cloth rustled behind him.

Burke whirled.

A tapestry had been flung back, revealing a previously-hidden door. Framed in it, well over seven feet tall, stood a creature Burke couldn't believe even now, as he stared at it.

The thing was a man, at first glance—a giant of a man, mightily muscled. He wore nothing save the traditional Minoan loin-band.

But it was the creature's head that held Burke; froze him.

For instead of a human head, to match a human body, this monster had the head of a gigantic bull, with monstrous horns and great glaring eyes and nostrils that flared and quivered.

Burke's hand shook so his lamp almost slopped over. A slow step at a time, he tried to back away.

But now, with a great bull-roar, the monster's head came down. It lunged at him.

Burke hurled the lamp at it.

Incredibly fast, the thing dodged. The lamp struck the wall. Flame leaped along the tapestry.

But the Minotaur paid the fire no heed. Again it lunged at Burke, spearing in at him with one of the great bull horns.

Barely in time, Burke dived aside. Desperately, he scrambled past the central tank, searching vainly for some weapon. When he stumbled over a low stool, he snatched it up, glad for anything that he could use to strike a blow.

Another bellow. The monster launched a new charge.

Burke swung the stool.

But even as the blow descended, the Minotaur brought up huge hands to stop it. Catching the stool by the legs, the creature jerked it up, trying to wrestle it away from Burke.

For an instant, then, they struggled, toe to toe, fighting for possession of the stool.

But only for an instant, for Burke knew without question what the outcome would be; must be. No ordinary man could stand against this hideous freak of nature. It simply was too much to hope for.

Yet unless he won, what would happen to Ariadne?

Fiercely, he threw all his weight onto the stool, swinging by it, completely clear of the floor.

Then, savagely, he slashed a foot down, so that the edge of his shoe raked his opponent's shin from knee to ankle before it hit the instep with smashing force.

The Minotaur half doubled over. A hoarse gust of pain burst from its throat.

Burke let go the stool. With all his might, he struck straight upward, between the monster's outstretched arms to the great bull-jaw.

New sounds of anguish—almost human, this time. The creature lurched forward flat-footed, off balance.

Burke leaped back. Catching the huge horns, he gave them a tremendous wrench, with all his weight behind it, the way he'd seen bull-doggers handle steers at rodeos.

Something cracked, so loud Burke could hear it even through the tumult. He wrenched again, harder.

A tearing sound, this time.

The next instant, Burke tumbled to the floor.

And that didn't make sense, because he still gripped the Minotaur's great horns.

Spasmodically, he threw himself to one side and over.

Across the room, the whole length of the tapestry was in flames now, blazing and crackling. Eddies of fire danced along the cypress beam above it, and the door-frame.

In front of it stood the Minotaur.

Only now, the Minotaur had no head.

At least, not the great bull's head. That was gone, torn away, left to lie like a hideous mask on the floor midway between Burke and the creature.

Where the bull's head had been, atop the monster's mighty shoulders was now, instead, a human head ... the tiny, distorted skull of a microcephalic imbecile.

And on top of that head—eyes glittering balefully; tentacles hugging it tight to its host's skull—squatted what appeared to be a jet-black octopus slightly less than the size of a bowling ball.

Yet it was no octopus sprung from Earth's own waters. Burke knew that the instant he saw it; knew it by the way the creature's eyes fixed on him; knew it in the chill that shook him as the thing's evil intelligence lanced forth to lock in mortal combat with him in his own brain.

And in a way, all that was good. At least, it relieved him of uncertainty; demonstrated once and for all that he'd been right when he refused to believe offspring could come from the mating of bull and woman.

No, that was only fable; a Bronze Age fantasy.

The fact, quite probably, was that Pasiphae had given birth to an imbecile who also happened by some strange quirk to be a physical giant.

What better host for an alien telepath, a creature not adapted to Earth as a planet or to dry-land living?

Then, to conceal the truth, hide alien and microcephalic skull alike beneath a great bull's head mask, and build a labyrinthine domicile where only its victims would ever meet it face to face.

All of which was interesting as conjecture, but hardly of practical use to a man faced with an alien-guided, seven-foot giant as of this very moment.

Such thoughts—! In spite of his plight, Burke couldn't help but smile wryly. With a strong effort of will, he forced the alien's probing tentacles of thought out of his brain; rose slowly, warily, holding the octopod's glittering eyes with his own.

He was on his feet now; and, once up, he became distinctly, unpleasantly aware of the room's heat ... the billows of smoke, the roaring of the flames that leaped along the roof-beams.

It was time for him to leave. Definitely.

For the fraction of a second, he let his eyes flicker towards the door.

Like a flash, his giant foe lunged for him. Before he could duck or dodge, he was jammed back against the wall. Great hands shoved at his chest, pinning him.

Desperately, Burke tried to strike back.

His reach was too short. He couldn't land a blow.

Now a vacuous smirk wreathed the microcephalic's loose-lipped face. The tiny eyes shone with delight.

There was no change in the octopod's baleful glare.

Now the giant pushed harder ... harder....

Burke felt his ribs begin to give. He swung his arms wildly, clutching in a frenzy for something—anything—

His hand touched an oil-jar. He clawed it to him.

But the Minotaur merely shifted, blocking him so he couldn't strike a blow.

Death was very close now. Burke knew it. Another moment, and his ribs would snap and pierce his heart, his lungs.

A convulsive tremor shook him. Oil spilled from the jar.

Oil—!

With his last ounce of strength, he brought the jar up sharply, knowing even as he did it that his foe would block the blow.

But the oil would keep on going, maybe....

It hit the alien full in the face.

Burke could feel the thing lose control of its host. Even in his own brain, it was as if a crushing weight had suddenly been lifted.

Simultaneously, the human giant's arms dropped.

Burke ducked and threw himself bodily at the other's knees.

The imbecile fell.

And now, alien abandoned host, racing across the floor on its tentacles towards the shimmering, blue-white tank.

Burke snatched up a second oil-jar; hurled its contents.

The oil slapped over the creature in a wave. Fire leaped from the flaming tapestry to meet it.

The next instant the alien itself was a threshing, blazing ball.

Then a ceiling timber crashed down on it in a shower of sparks.

The threshing stopped.

Burke ran for the nearest door....

CHAPTER VIII

She wasn't there. Even when he ran back through her rooms, calling her name aloud, she wasn't there.

Numbly, Burke stumbled forth again, out onto the long ascending ramp that led to the central court.

Over on the far side, at the Shrine of Oracles, orange-yellow flames leaped high into the black night sky. Whipped by the buffeting south wind, they jumped to another building while Burke watched; then on to still another. Silhouetted figures ran this way and that—gesturing, shouting.

Once again, Burke checked his watch.

Eleven fifty-five now. Only five brief minutes till the moment all Knossos was to be destroyed, according to the time inverter's scanner screen.

Still Burke hesitated, straining his eyes against the night as he strove for some glimpse of Ariadne. In taut concentration, he listened for the distant echo of her voice.

Without avail.

Then, while he yet lingered, a man called out to him hoarsely. He wheeled just as one of Minos' huge Sudani guards came hurrying in his direction.

It was a stimulus Burke couldn't ignore. Another moment and the man might recognize him. Whirling, he sprinted up the nearest stairway, then across the flat roof of the back of the building.

A quick drop to the ground again. A daredevil slide down the steep East Bastion. A stumbling, headlong run along the bank of the river called Kairatos to the cover of a clump of cypress trees.

But now that he had started running, it seemed the best idea not to stop. On he fled, and on, clambering over boulders, careening into ditches.

Then, at last, he found himself in a crown of brush atop a little knoll, a good half-mile or better from the palace. Panting, unable to go further, Burke flung himself down in the blackest of the shadows and lay there, staring back at the strange, stark majesty that was Knossos.

The flames of the fire he'd started in the Labyrinth still were spreading. Sparks swirled in the wind, carried high by blaze-stoked updrafts; then dispersed, floating farther and farther from the central core of heat, till at last they fell again, to ignite new buildings.

Tearing his attention from the distant holocaust, Burke peered at his watch once more.

Twelve ten.

So the zero hour had come and gone, with nothing happening save the continued spread of the fire.

Burke felt a little sick. Had all his efforts, his anguish, gone for nothing? Was he to live out his life in Bronze Age Crete to no purpose save to prove correct that part of Pendlebury's theory that said that Knossos, dying, had been swept by fire?

Burke cursed beneath his breath. He still couldn't, wouldn't, believe it. It left too many loopholes. After all, what about the business of the radiation traces he'd detected; the blighted circle that showed on the scanner screen? Why, for so many hundred years, had Cretans shunned the site of their ancient glory?

Then, too there were his own personal experiences of the past few hours to think of. Pasiphae's monstrous imbecile son; the octopodal alien telepath— what roles did they play?

Not to mention the great, shimmering, blue-white ship hidden deep within the earth.

Certainly Pendlebury's theory offered little save the detail of the fire to commend it. The invasion part, the idea that outsiders had swept down on the palace with torch and sword—that simply wasn't true.

Not unless he, Dion Burke, might be said to constitute a whole task force in himself, just because by accident he'd set the Labyrinth ablaze.

As for his hopes, his dreams, the way he felt towards Ariadne—

A wave of sheer frustration came with the thought. Savagely, Burke hammered the dirt with a clenched fist. Then, breathing hard, he scrambled to his feet.

Only in that same moment, a sound pulsed in upon him ... a high, thin, wailing sound that rose in sudden sharp crescendo.

Burke spun round.

But before he could even place the noise, the earth beneath his feet began to shake. A roar, louder and deeper than the bellow of a thousand angry bulls, thundered up to counterpoint the wail.

Simultaneously, light flared, so blinding bright Burke had to throw up his arms to shield his eyes.

The glare seemed to come from the southeast, off in the direction where Mount Lasithi's rocky pinnacles rose.

Mount Lasithi, whose towering, cliff-girt bastions shielded the sacred Cave of Zeus....

While Burke cringed, the radiance seemed to fade a little. The earth-shaking roar diminished also. The shrill wail struck a slightly less ear-piercing note.

Another moment, and Burke dared to squint skyward once more.

What he saw made the hair stand up along the back of his neck.

For off there, to the southeast, a great spray of light radiated out from Mount Lasithi. Before his very eyes, the whole crest seemed to split asunder. Rocky buttresses crumbled. Great crags and ledges split away.

Up from among them rose a huge, flattened, metallic cone—the blue-white ship at which Burke had stared in awe brief hours before.

Light pulsed from it now, as if it were a miniature sun. Rock fell away from the craft in avalanches as it broke free of the mountain.

Now the light drew into a single, broad, fan-shaped shaft that thrust down from the ship's base to the rugged terrain of the shattered mountain below. The thing began to climb, faster and faster.

Then, as it gained altitude, it swung round in a tremendous, wheeling circle ... swung round, and then straightened, and lanced earthward once more, straight for the flaming tumult that was Knossos.

Burke threw himself flat in the dirt.

It was wasted caution. He might as well not have been there. The alien ship went wide of him by miles.

Another moment, and it was hovering over Knossos; leveling off till its base was parallel to the ground below.

Slowly, slowly, then it descended, riding down on its fan-shaped shaft of light till it hung bare feet above the tops of the buildings. For an instant, Burke thought it must surely be going to land.

But no. For suddenly, the light-shaft pulsed brighter by a dozen, a hundred, a thousand times. The ship spun in a low, flat circle that carried it over the entire area of the palace and surrounding grounds in seconds.

Then the wailing sound went shrill again—so shrill Burke clapped his hands over his ears. The ship peeled away from the palace and lanced into the sky like an electron-streak. In a flash, it was gone—gone from Knossos, from Crete, from Earth itself ... a dim and distant pinpoint, sparkling as it faded away, incredibly fast, into the night.

Numbly, Burke turned once more to the palace.

So far as he could see from this vantage-point, no sign of life remained. It was as if a giant hammer had smashed down on it; reduced it to a heap of tumbled stone. Even the fires were dead.

And Ariadne—?

Burke couldn't let himself think about her. Better to marvel at the alien ship, with its pulsing power that shattered mountains and wiped out cities. Better to grope for some bitter tendril of satisfaction that at last he'd learned the truth about the palace's destruction.

As if that would do him any good now.

Because always, always, fight as he might against it, Ariadne was in his mind and heart alike.

Yet perhaps she'd survived. After all, he'd not been able to find her in her quarters. And she'd promised to meet him—where was it?—on the headland to the left of the mouth of the River of Amnissus.

At least, hunting for her would give him something to do; something to occupy his muscles and maybe, even, a small part of his brain.

So, now, he rose; turned towards the sea.

It was nearly dawn before he found his way to the headland. By then, the wind had died, and the sky in the east lay grey as the whispering, slate-colored waves.

A spark of tension came to life within Burke. Suddenly eager, heedless of fatigue, he clawed his way to the headland's highest point and scanned the whole area.

No sign of Ariadne.

The spark flickered; died. Dully, Burke stared out across the shadowy sea.

His life from now on would be like that: grey; all grey.

It didn't even matter that now he could see the hidden pattern behind the rise of Bronze Age Crete.

The alien ship's presence was, of course, the key.

Obviously, that ship had brought the biggest part of so-called Minoan culture with it. That was why Cretan civilization had flowered so incredibly fast. Perhaps even the Minoans themselves had arrived on Earth aboard the craft, as dry-land slaves in the service of masters better adapted to a liquid environment.

Why had the aliens come? That was a question harder to answer. But whether because of external foes or internal problems, the creatures had been looking for a new world to colonize. And since the Mediterranean teemed with octopi, Cephalopoda, no doubt Crete had offered advantages. Maybe there'd been experiments—attempts to cross-breed the superior, telepathic aliens with the less-highly-developed native octopi. Or perhaps the intruders had merely sought to adapt themselves to life in water, rather than the smelly stuff in the Labyrinth tank.

In any case, they'd held Crete for a long, long time—the way they'd buried their ship in the heart of Mount Lasithi proved that.

Minos, in turn, had played the role of a Quisling, power-hungry intermediary between his own race and the aliens. To hold his kingship, he'd had Daedalus build the Labyrinth, to serve as quarters for the alien overseer who, in the guise of oracle, held final power in Knossos. And when a human host for this octopodal commandant had been demanded— a man to serve as transportation for the creature—Minos had blackened his wife's name and dedicated his imbecile son to the duty.

Or perhaps he hadn't. Perhaps he'd done the things he'd done reluctantly, and only in order to save his people from alien wrath such as had struck tonight.

In any case, the death of the alien in the Labyrinth had served as trigger for the disaster. One of their number slain, the extraterrestrials no doubt had concluded Earth unsafe, and so had fled back to the outer space from which they'd come.

Which meant that the alien's slayer was also responsible for Knossos' fall ... the death that had struck down all the hundreds trapped in the now-blighted palace area tonight.

Burke shivered.

Only there was another side to that, too.

For instance, suppose he'd stayed in his own time; never come to Crete, nor slain the Minotaur?

Where would that leave Earth? As an alien outpost, overrun with telepathic octopodal horrors, while Man survived as mere serfs to carry out the bidding of the master race?

Again, questions without answers.

Burke's shoulders shook.

But then, while he still stood brooding—fatigue-worn, lame, half-sick—the first pale fingers of the sun began to touch the horizon with rose.

Turning, Burke stared down at the river and the tiny port village near its mouth.

As if his move had been a signal, there was a sudden stir of activity. Men hurried to and fro along the water's edge. A Greek long ship pushed out from shore.

Now those aboard the craft hoisted its sail.

A black sail.

Involuntarily, Burke stiffened.

Because the black sail made it Theseus' ship.

And legend said Theseus left Crete with Ariadne.

Burke ran for the point closest to the water; stared tight-lipped at the long, slim vessel.

Scarlet caught his eye—the scarlet of a woman's bright-striped cloak.

The same cloak Ariadne had swirled for him so prettily, perhaps—?

Burke dived from his point, straight down into the river. With all his strength, he swam to intercept the slowly-drifting long ship.

Now those aboard had glimpsed him. Men pointed. Women's voices rose, thin on the morning breeze.

Burke plowed the water closer ... closer....

And now a brawny, familiar figure came striding to the bow: Theseus, Hero of Athens.

Burke swam the harder. Just a dozen strokes more—

Almost, it seemed as if he could reach out and touch Theseus.

The Athenian leaned forward—face stiff, teeth bared, eyes bright with malice. Then his arm came up and back, and Burke saw he gripped a spear.

Theseus hurled the weapon in the same instant.

Desperately, Burke tried to throw himself aside.

But the waves, the water, slowed his movements. The spear struck home, deep in his shoulder.

In spite of himself, Burke cried out.

And now Theseus caught up another spear and poised to throw it.

Burke drove the air from his lungs in a gust. He sank like a rock, turning over and over, as the rush of the Amnissus into the sea carried him along.

But at least there were no more spears; and after a long moment when it seemed his lungs must surely burst, he fought his way back to the surface, and drank in air, and then floated till he could grit his teeth and tear Theseus' javelin from his shoulder.

After that, there was the long swim back to shore—a swim against the current, this time. By the time Burke made it, Theseus' ship was toy-size in the distance.

For his own part, and what with fatigue and pain and loss of blood, Burke wasn't at all sure that he cared whether he lived or died. Stumbling up from the water onto a narrow strip of beach, he crumpled face-down before he'd gone ten steps.

Half in delirium, thinking of Ariadne, he almost sobbed aloud.

The delirium grew. He knew it did, because now he could even hear her calling to him dimly, as from afar.

Only then the voice came closer: "Dion, Dion! Please, my lord Dion, speak to me!"

Hands lifted his head; cradled it in soft arms. Tender fingers smoothed his hair and brushed the sand from his face.

With a tremendous effort, Burke opened his eyes.

And there was Ariadne.

It took him a full minute to know he wasn't dreaming, or in that dark half-world between reality and hallucination.

Then, at last, incredibly, it was true, and she was with him, her salt tears spattering his face faster than she could wipe them away. "Oh, my lord Dion ..." she whispered, again and again, "My Dion, my Dion!"

Burke said hoarsely, "Ariadne, what happened? I thought—How'd you get here?"

"How indeed, my lord Dion!" Of a sudden the slim princess was laughing through her tears. "I walked, as you did, though it took me longer, for I wanted to be sure we were free of that dog Theseus before I joined you."

"Free of Theseus—?"

"Of course. When he came seeking me at my quarters in the night I fled, then followed him, till I knew for certain he was aboard his ship."

And that brought up another matter: "But—the cloak—the woman—"

"The woman?" Never had Ariadne looked more a picture of wide-eyed innocence. "I do not understand, my lord."

Burke gave her back stare for stare, holding his tongue; and after a moment, with a sound suspiciously like a giggle, she murmured, "It could not be my maid you mean, could it, my lord?"

"Your maid—?"

"Yes, the peasant girl who found such favor with Theseus." Ariadne's dark eyes held more than a hint of laughter. "I thought it only fitting that he be rewarded for his efforts, Lord Dion. So I wrapped the wench in my cloak and told her that if she kept her face hidden and played the role of Princess Ariadne long enough and well enough, she might end up as Theseus' queen."

The picture was perfect. Burke laughed till he feared he'd open his wound again.

Ariadne laughed with him for a moment, then sobered. "I meant what I told her, Lord Dion. She's a clever girl, and Theseus can see no farther than the nearest bed. By the time he reaches Athens, she may have him so in her toils as not to be able to bear the thought of parting from her."

Burke smiled wryly; shook his head. "I'm sorry, Ariadne. It won't work. Theseus isn't going to like being tricked. So when he puts in at Naxos, he'll leave your maid behind."

Ariadne's great eyes widened. "And—Theseus himself—?"

"When he reaches Athens, he'll find his father dead."

"I see." The slim, lovely princess nodded slowly. "And then, you'll go to Athens, and you'll kill him. And after that, if my father, Minos, still lives, you'll kill him, too. And then—"

Burke said, "No, princess."

"No—?" she stared. "What do you mean?"

"I mean, I'm all through killing."

Burke shifted, trying to ease his wound. "You see, Ariadne, I don't need to kill anyone. Because Theseus isn't stupid, really, and after all this trouble here, he's going to settle down and make Athens a good king.

"As for your father, he's alive. But we don't need to worry any more about him. All he's thinking of is avenging himself on Daedalus for helping us. Only Daedalus is going to get away to the court of King Cocalus, in Sicily, and Cocalus' daughter will kill Minos."

It was a long speech. When he'd finished, Ariadne brought up her hands and crossed them on her firm, bared breasts. "It is good to know what the future holds, my lord Dionysus. I thank you."

Quick irritation touched Burke. "Damn it, girl, I'm not—"

He stopped short.

That line he'd half spoken—the one about him not being Dionysus, not a god; just plain Dion Burke?

Was it true, really?

After all, in a world as primitive as this, what was a god but a man who knew spectacularly more than his fellows?

So, wasn't Ariadne maybe right? Wasn't the Dionysus of legend maybe just plain Dion Burke, twentieth century man, set down in Bronze Age Crete with his name corrupted to fit the language and the era?

And in that case—

Ariadne squirmed a little and began to smooth his hair again. Her hand trembled, ever so slightly. Her voice, too. She whispered, "My lord, this talk of days to come—would you tell me about—about—"

"About you, you mean? About your own future?"

Ariadne hid her face. Her words came tremulous and muffled. "Yes, yes, my lord!"

Burke couldn't help but smile a little. It was a good thing he practically knew his classical mythology by heart.

And there was nothing quite like time travel to make a man's predictions work out.

Shifting, he brought his good arm up so he could hold Ariadne. Then, very gently, he began: "You needn't fear, my princess. You and I—we'll go to

Lemnos, make our home there. Then, we'll have four children—Thoas, Staphylus, Oenopion, Peparthus...."

It was a good story, even if somewhat foreshortened by the fact that Ariadne stopped it with her lips.

Then, abruptly, she halted the new activity, too, saying, "My lord Dionysus, Lemnos is a far place. We'd better try to find a ship before the sun climbs higher into the sky."

Together, they got up, then, and moved slowly down the beach towards the tiny harbor town.

As for the sun, Burke decided it had never shone on a finer day.

www.ingramcontent.com/pod-product-compliance
Ingram Content Group UK Ltd.
Pitfield, Milton Keynes, MK11 3LW, UK
UKHW031834270325
456796UK00003B/444